Nature Is Enough

Nature Is Enough

Religious Naturalism and the Meaning of Life

Loyal Rue

Published by State University of New York Press, Albany

For information, contact State University of New York Press, Albany, NY
www.sunypress.edu

Production by Eileen Meehan
Marketing by Anne M. Valentine

Library of Congress Cataloging-in-Publication Data

Rue, Loyal D.
  Nature is enough : religious naturalism and the meaning of life / Loyal Rue.
        p. cm.
  Includes bibliographical references (p.   ) and index.
  ISBN 978-1-4384-3800-9 (paperback : alk. paper)
  ISBN 978-1-4384-3799-6 (hardcover : alk. paper)
    1. Nature—Religious aspects.   2. Naturalism—Religious aspects.   I. Title.

  BL65.N35R84 2011   2011003136
  211'.8—dc22

                         10 9 8 7 6 5 4 3 2 1

In memory of
Philemon Sturges
(*bon vivant*)

Contents

Contents

Preface

This book results from a conflation of two abandoned projects: one about religious naturalism and the other about the meaning of life.

For several years I have identified myself as a religious naturalist without having any clear conception of what religious naturalism actually amounts to. I had long since abandoned the metaphysics of supernaturalism, but still retained what I recognized to be religious sensibilities. So I must have been, by default, a religious naturalist. I knew of several others who had taken up the label but, like me, none of them had elaborated its major themes in a systematic way. Eventually I took in mind to edit a book under the title *Is Nature Enough?* The idea was to enlist several well-known thinkers to weigh in on both sides of the question. My hope was that the positive responses to the question would provide the initial statements from which an articulate movement might begin to flourish. So I assembled a wish list of flashy thinkers that I knew would make substantial contributions. At the top of the list was (of course) Stephen Hawking. I then sent Hawking a carefully worded invitation to contribute an article in response to the question. I wasn't exactly mortified when he graciously declined my invitation, but I was sufficiently discouraged to give up on the project. Then, a few months after I had abandoned the book project, my friend and fellow religious naturalist, Michael Cavanaugh, informed me that he was organizing a conference around the question. One of the presenters at the conference was theologian John Haught, who responded negatively to the question, and who has since published a book under the title *Is Nature Enough?*[1] I mention this because the present book is in some measure a response to Haught's objections to religious naturalism.

The other abandoned project concerned the meaning of life. I had taken a scholarly interest in this topic partly because it was beginning to show up as a standard feature in introductory philosophy textbooks, but also because it is one of very few topics that has attracted the attention of a broad range of philosophers and theologians. So I decided to offer a seminar on the topic as a way of forcing myself to undertake a thorough review of the material. I had initially settled on the idea of writing something on the meaning of life, but in the process of working through the literature I concluded that it was pretty decent stuff, and that I had nothing clever or interesting to add to it. So that appeared to be the end of that.

Having abandoned both religious naturalism and the meaning of life, I turned to the next item on my list of things to look into: *emergence theory*. The topic of emergence had attracted the attention of some interesting and important thinkers, and was no longer merely a sophisticated way of saying "Then *presto!*; that happened." The contemporary concept of emergence is embedded in chaos and complexity theory—very edgy and speculative stuff, but full of exciting potential. In the process of working through the literature on emergence theory it came to me that here was a resource for framing questions about the meaning of life in a new way. And it also struck me that emergence theory provided the right kind of footing for articulating a contemporary vision of religious naturalism.

The present book is an attempt to unearth these abandoned projects and to bring them together under the thesis that if religious naturalism deserves to be taken at all seriously it must have a satisfying answer to the question of meaningful human existence. If it does, then it might be fairly claimed that nature is enough.

The ambitions of this book are modest, and the plan is uncomplicated. The introductory chapter takes a bearing on the question of the meaning of life and then sets down three conditions that must be met for a human life to be considered genuinely meaningful. One of these conditions—the teleological criterion—raises what is perhaps the most bothersome issue for any serious quest to apprehend the meaning of life: Is the meaning of life—the goal, the purpose, the point of life—an objective thing that might be discovered, or is it merely an invention that humans construct for their own personal or political convenience? In other words, is the meaning of life a reality or an illusion? I take the view that we are left with four distinct options for thinking about the reality of meaning, and these options are explored in the two chapters comprising Part One. Part Two then tries to show how a naturalistic perspective on the meaning of life might contribute to a contemporary vision of the religious life. Here it will be asked whether a naturalist might possibly be religious and, if so, what that might actually look like.

1

Introduction

What Is a Human Being For?

Questioning the Question

For several years I have made a practice of subjecting my introductory philosophy students to a pop quiz on the first day of class. The assignment is to write an essay in response to a simple question: "What is a human being for?" This is obviously a variation on the more familiar question, "What is the meaning of life?" But the form of the question is sufficiently odd to leave students in a state of bewilderment. They know perfectly well what chairs and cups and backpacks are for, but it has never occurred to them that human beings might be *for anything* in a similar way. An odd question, perhaps, but eventually the students manage to compose themselves with varied and predictable results. A human being is for:

> Learning and solving problems
> Preserving and beautifying the earth
> Serving God
> Loving and being loved
> Whatever they choose to be for
> Realizing their potential
> Survival and reproduction
> Feeding decomposers
> Etc.

I engage students in this exercise because it gives them a whiff of the sort of questions that might come up in philosophy, and also because it gives me a whiff of the values and attitudes I will encounter during the course of the semester. Yet it must be admitted that asking students to answer this question on the first day of class is a particularly unphilosophical thing to do. This is because the first step in philosophy is always to scrutinize questions, not to answer them. Indeed, one of my own college professors used to insist that philosophy has no business answering questions at all, but should confine itself to rendering critiques of questions.

Is the Question Answerable?

Before we can hope to make any progress on the question about life's meaning we must determine whether the question itself is problematic. Many questions are. Some questions are problematic because they are unanswerable, either because they are incoherent or because we lack sufficient means to answer them. For example, take the old standard from theology: Can God create a stone too heavy for God to lift? This question was designed to demonstrate that God cannot possibly be omnipotent. If we say that God *can* create such a stone, then it follows that there is one thing God is powerless to do: namely, to lift the stone. But if we admit that God *cannot* create the stone, then ipso facto God is not omnipotent. Any answer to the question implies that God is not all-powerful. On the surface this question has the appearance of legitimacy, but in fact the question is incoherent because it creates a logical monstrosity: a stone too heavy to be lifted by a being presumed capable of lifting any stone at all amounts to a logically impossible stone.

Some philosophers have maintained that the meaning of life question is incoherent in a similar way, not because it creates a logical monstrosity but because it creates a grammatical one. Ludwig Wittgenstein, for example, believed that human life is the context of meaning—the setting wherein things take on meaning—and cannot therefore be a candidate for meaning itself.[1] By this reasoning, to inquire about the meaning of life is absurd in the way that voting for the voting booth would be. Wittgenstein's suggestion that our question is illegitimate rests on the claim that it is a recursive question of the sort, "What is the meaning of this question?" But is it? It is not obvious that "What is the meaning of life?" constitutes the same kind of grammatical monstrosity as "What is the meaning of this question?" Does the fact that entities and events in life can have meaning imply that it makes no sense to ask whether a life itself can have meaning? It's hard to see why. It seems perfectly sensible to ask, "What is the color of the box containing red things?" If there is no logical or grammatical monstrosity in that question, then it seems logically and grammatically permissible to inquire about the meaning of life.

It appears, then, that our question is not rendered unanswerable on grounds of incoherence. It might, however, be unanswerable on other grounds. Some questions are theoretically impossible to answer. Heisenberg's uncertainty principle tells us it is impossible to determine both the velocity and the location of an elementary particle at the same time. A choice to observe one necessarily prevents observation of the other. Similarly, it may be that the meaning of life is just inaccessible in principle. If it were supposed, for example, that knowing the meaning of life required information that has been irretrievably lost, then it would be futile to pursue an answer. Or consider the possibility that the question is unanswerable due to our own limitations. When asked about the existence of God, one of Woody Allen's characters dismissed the question with, "How should I know? I get lost in Chinatown." Perhaps the meaning of life is like that—no matter how desperately we need the answer it might be completely over our heads. Contemporary physicists find themselves in this condition with respect to quantum theory. They use the theory as a tool all the time, and with impressive results, but they do not pretend to comprehend it. As Richard Feynman famously quipped, "I think I can safely say that no one understands quantum mechanics." If we are incapable of comprehending even the simplest events in nature, then what makes us think we can comprehend the meaning of life?

Another of my college professors used to say that philosophy amounts to a series of questions that cannot be answered, but *must* be answered. Like quantum physicists, perhaps, we might manage to get on in life even though its true meaning is forever beyond us. This may very well be the case, but the fact remains that no one has yet *shown* it to be so. We have no equivalent to Heisenberg's uncertainty principle that can be applied to the meaning of life. And without such a demonstration we need not feel compelled to dismiss the question as unanswerable—at least not before completing our attempt to see more clearly what sort of question it is.

Is the Question Misleading?

A question may be problematic even though it is legitimate and answerable. Our question, "What is the meaning of life?" appears to be misleading in problematic ways. A question would be misleading if it made unwarranted assumptions, or if it were ambiguous. For example, the question, "Who is the emperor of New York?" is obviously misinformed because it makes the false assumption that there *is* an emperor of New York. It appears that our question makes a similar assumption: it asks about the meaning of life as if it were obvious that life *has* meaning. But this is certainly not obvious to everyone. In fact, many would object to the assumption, insisting that "What is the meaning of life?" should be read to ask, "*Is* there any meaning to life?" In the pages ahead it will be important to keep both readings of the question firmly in mind. We might accomplish this by reformulating the question to read: "Does life have meaning, and if so, what is it?"

But even this reformulation of the question is misleading because it assumes that the meaning of life is singular and objective. Many people may be satisfied with (and even insist upon) the assumption that there is a one-size-fits-all meaning to life, but others would find reasons to object strenuously. Some, for example, might insist on a distinction between multiple meanings *in* life and a singular meaning *of* life. The fact that many particular things in a person's life may be meaningful in various ways does not make it obvious that life in general is meaningful. We have already seen that Wittgenstein's objection relies on this distinction. He believed that things *in* life could be found meaningful, but that it made no sense to ask whether life itself is meaningful.

Of course, it might make sense—Wittgenstein notwithstanding—to affirm the meaning of life as a whole if we assume that it is derived from particular meanings in life. When I say, in a general sense, that I enjoy my mother's cooking I mean that I find a majority of her meals enjoyable. Analogously, a person might judge that life as a whole is meaningful simply because it contains an abundance of objects, events, and relations that are themselves meaningful. But if this is the case, then we might extend the same principle to declare that life as a whole is always meaningful in a potential sense, regardless of whether it contains particular meanings. For example, if I reject the meaningfulness of life as a whole because I find nothing in life particular meaningful, you might respond by accusing me of a failure of insight or imagination, and insist that I would find life meaningful if only I got my thinking straight. The meaning of life in this sense would be grounded in the perpetual possibility for meaningfulness, that is, the meaning may be found, whether or not we succeed in finding it.

It should be apparent that our question may be misleading in various ways, and for that reason we must take care to clarify our assumptions along the way and to identify any possible ambiguities.

The following variations on our question illustrate just how open the question is to multiple readings:

> Why is there anything at all, rather than nothing?
> What is the purpose of creation?
> Why should I go on living?
> How should I live my life?
> Does anything matter?
> What is the nature of the life process?

Is the Question Authentic?

Rhetorical questions are generally taken to be inauthentic. They merely pretend to be questions, whereas they are really assertions or exclamations masquerading as questions. "What are friends for?" really means "*This* is what friends are for!" If I were to ask whether you had purchased a lottery ticket and you responded, "What's the point?" I would not consider telling you that the point is to win a lot of money. We both know perfectly well what the point of entering the lottery is. Rather, your rhetorical question is really a commentary on the folly of wagering good money against bad odds.

Perhaps questions about the meaning of life are not genuine questions at all, but merely veiled complaints, or expressions of confusion, or pleas for sympathy. We have good reason to expect that questions about the meaning of life will be far more likely to arise in the context of adversity or uncertainty. Suppose your neighbor has just lost her family in a senseless accident and cries out, "What's the point of existing?" In this case it would be foolish to suppose that she is expressing an interest in doing some serious reading in philosophy. That would be the farthest thing from her mind. The point here is that the adverse circumstances in which questions about the meaning of life frequently arise might suggest that such questions are intended for effect, in which case they would be rhetorical questions and therefore not genuine.

Questions about the meaning of life may in fact often be rhetorical, but there is no reason to accept the view that they are always or even primarily so. The question might just as well arise in a philosophy class, or on vacation, or in a supermarket. But even if the question is used rhetorically it remains a serious and important one. It would be a grave error to conclude that the significance of questions may always be reduced to their particular contexts. In the case of our grief stricken neighbor the question may have taken the form of an emotional outburst, but this does not imply that it lacks independent merit as a legitimate intellectual inquiry. It would be easy to assume that the poor woman is just not thinking clearly in the circumstances and that nothing she says should be taken seriously. But maybe she is thinking more clearly than ever; maybe her loss is the occasion for her deepest insights about the meaning of life. Perhaps the emotional force behind the outburst should be seen not as invalidating the question, but rather as providing strong warrant for taking it seriously in the intellectual sense.

Is It a Philosophical Question?

Not all questions are philosophically significant. Our question about the meaning of life might qualify as answerable, coherent and authentic but still be lacking in philosophical interest. According to a popular conception of philosophy, the meaning of life shows up as the quintessential philosophical problem. Readers of the *New Yorker* may take this impression from cartoons featuring a philosophical sage seated on a mountaintop (or in a cave) receiving seekers after the meaning of existence. But this popular impression is slightly misleading, for it turns out that relatively few philosophers have bothered to address the question directly, and a majority would agree that the meaning of life is no more central to philosophy than questions that arise within science, politics, religion, and the arts.

Traditionally, philosophy has concerned itself with three principal problem areas: epistemology (the foundations, scope, and limits of knowledge), metaphysics (the ultimate nature of reality), and value theory (the grounds and norms for ethics and aesthetics). Any inquiry becomes philosophical to the extent that it traffics in one or more of these problem areas, which our question appears to do. For example, it is not self-evident that the meaning of life can be known, so any assertion or assumption one way or the other must be supported by argument, and to provide such arguments is to engage in epistemology. The same holds for metaphysical assertions and assumptions. Many discussions of the meaning of life posit (or reject) the existence of God, or immortality of the soul, or freedom of the will, or a universal purpose—all of which involve metaphysical commitments and argumentation. And finally, philosophers have occasionally tried to show that inquiry into the meaning of life does not ask for metaphysical explanation at all, but merely seeks a justification to show that life is worth living. But any attempt to provide (or critique) such justifications places the inquiry squarely in the domain of value theory.

It appears, then, that the meaning of life qualifies as a legitimate concern for philosophy, but it should be emphasized that while the question is sufficiently philosophical it is neither central nor exclusive to the discipline. In the chapters ahead I will not assume that the question of life's meaning belongs exclusively to philosophy, yet it is one that should be extensively vetted by philosophical critique. In particular, philosophy should be able to provide some guidance in shaping the question. But perhaps even more importantly, philosophy might help to clarify what is meant by "meaning."

The Meaning of Meaning

The meanings of words and the significance of objects and events are normally taken for granted. It is only when problems arise, when we fail to apprehend or to express meaning, that the nature of meaning becomes an issue. If this is so, then important clues to what we *mean* when we declare that life is meaningful might be found where meaning is conspicuously absent.

Consider der *Muselmann*

Human existence was scraped raw in the Nazi death camps of World War II. Conditions in the camps were carefully constructed for the systematic degradation of human lives. The majority of prisoners lived in absolute squalor, forced to endure terror, uncertainty, humiliation, hunger, fatigue, frostbite, disease, and injury, while constantly facing the threat of extermination. Anything resembling faith, hope, charity, or a sense of dignity would, under these circumstances, bear the mark of unreason. Fear, disgust, resentment, suspicion, and an overwhelming sense of injustice prevailed. Having lost their will to live, many prisoners exercised the option for suicide, but most somehow found the means to struggle on, one terrifying day at a time.

A remnant of these Holocaust victims survived the death camps to produce a chilling literature of testimony, recording unthinkable atrocities and their impact upon victims. Strangely enough, the most disturbing figures among holocaust victims are given relatively little attention in the testimonial literature. These were *die Muselmänner.*[2] *Der Muselmann* was the ultimate victim of the death camps: a mere cipher, a zombie, a profoundly dehumanized nonperson. Jean Amery describes *der Muselmann* as "the prisoner who was giving up and was given up by his comrades, [he] no longer had room in his consciousness for the contrasts of good or bad, noble or base, intellectual or unintellectual. He was a staggering corpse, a bundle of physical functions in its last convulsions."[3] Ryn and Klodzinski render the following horrific picture of *der Muselmann*:

> The SS man was walking slowly, looking at the [*Muselmann*] who was coming toward him. We looked to the left, to see what would happen. Dragging his wooden clogs, the dull-witted and aimless creature ended up bumping right into the SS officer, who yelled at him and gave him a lashing on the head. The [*Muselmann*] stood still, without realizing what had happened. When he received a second and, then, a third lashing because he had forgotten to take off his cap, he began to do it on himself, as he had dysentery. When the SS man saw the black, stinking liquid begin to cover his clogs, he went crazy. He hurled himself on top of the [*Muselmann*] and began kicking his stomach with all his strength. Even after the poor thing had fallen into his own excrement, the SS man kept beating his head and chest. The [*Muselmann*] didn't defend himself. With the first kick, he folded in two, and after a few more he was dead.[4]

Der Muselmann was literally insensible, indifferent to his environment, beyond compliance or resistance, beyond the ability to care or take interest, beyond attraction or repulsion, beyond anticipation or memory, beyond the reach of information. Their faces rigid masks, their motions unintended, they sometimes crouched or stood shivering, what little behavior they performed was random, not owned. And yet they were living creatures.

The image of *der Muselmann* forces upon us questions about the meaning of life, and in a sense it also provides us with a vague measure of meaning, for in *der Muselmann* we encounter a mode of human existence that is uniquely and profoundly devoid of meaning. In the most general sense, therefore, it may be seen that the meaning of life is found in whatever constitutes the essential difference between *der Muselmann* and the rest of humanity.

How, then, shall we think about this essential difference? What sense can we make of phrases such as "living dead" and "staggering corpse"? In what sense is *der Muselmann* alive, and in what sense is he no longer meaningfully alive? In the most basic terms possible we may say that a living organism becomes a dead thing when its rate of chemical composition is overtaken by the rate of chemical decomposition. An organism dies when it becomes a plaything of environmental circumstances, when it no longer resists being absorbed into its environment by the pitiless forces of material recycling, when the distinction between self and world ceases to be. Living organisms are alive by virtue of complex dynamics that enable them to construct and maintain this vital distinction. In humans these dynamics are staggeringly complex, involving many interrelated systems and subsystems, all participating in a tightly scripted orchestration of countless cells.

If we apply this crude definition strictly we must agree that *der Muselmann* is technically alive because he continues, albeit inadvertently, to resist decomposition. He breathes, he metabolizes, he shivers from the cold, and so on. But this is merely to say that various subfunctions (i.e., reflex systems) remain intact. As much could be said of *der Muselmann* if we extracted various organs and sent them off to hospitals around the world, there to be kept ticking over by artificial means. The real question, however, is whether there is anything about *der Muselmann* that has the wherewithal to arouse the entire organism and to engage it in meaningful activity. *Der Muselmann's* heart continues to perform a subfunction, as do his kidneys, lungs, intestines, etc. But in the most decisive sense *der Muselmann* has become a plaything of his environment, a mere object that wants not, fears not, hopes not, thinks not. He is a human being merely by virtue of momentum. But there is no integrated striving, no attitude, no thesis, no person.

The Logic of Meaning

The bottom line in all of this is to say that the life of *der Muselmann* is no longer *about* anything. If something—a word, an object, an activity—has meaning, then it has the property of "aboutness." Our questions are, therefore, how human lives come to be about anything, and whether we can say with any confidence what they should be about.

Aboutness is a vague notion, suggesting an orientation or disposition of one thing toward another. The notion becomes only slightly more clear when we specify what sorts of things might have the property of aboutness.[5] Linguistic expressions (e.g., words, phrases, signs) have aboutness in an intuitively obvious sense. The word "apple," for example, is about a particular kind of fruit, just as "the Big Apple" is about a particular American city. The question, "where is the post office?" is about a certain building having a particular function, but it is also about the location of that building. States of mind, such as ideas, memories, and emotions have aboutness too. Your memories are about events and experiences that happened in the past, whereas your fears and hopes are about events and experiences that may happen in the future. Acts of behavior are directly or indirectly about the outcomes they are intended to produce. Even sensations and perceptions may be said to possess the property of aboutness. Your seeing or hearing is manifestly about whatever you see or hear, even when you aren't yet sure what the object or the sound is. And if a human life has meaning then it, too, must be about something or another.

Aboutness is one of several concepts that may be grouped together, by a sort of family resemblance, under the larger concept of teleology. Aboutness, functionality, representation, intentionality, value, and meaningfulness are all teleological terms. That is, they involve some *telos* (plural: *telē*), some end, goal, or purpose. There are subtle and important differences between each of these notions, but in the most general sense they all participate in the logic of means-to-end. Inherent in each of these concepts is the idea that something exists "for the sake of" something else. Teleological events—a behavior, for example—happen *so that* some future state might be achieved. The future state is the goal, the point, the value, the meaning of the behavior. If an event is genuinely teleological (goal governed), then we may say that it will not become fully intelligible until we identify the goal served by the behavior, what the behavior is *for*. Non-teleological events, by contrast, may be rendered intelligible by identifying *because of* factors, that is, antecedent causal conditions that operate aimlessly, without any suggestion of serving a purpose or function.

To illustrate: suppose we witness a brick falling loose from the top of a building. The falling of the brick may be rendered intelligible by reference to the laws of classical physics. We say the event happened *because of* various factors and forces, such as structural faults, gravity, and so on. But there is no *so that* story to be told. Now suppose we see a person falling from the building. The physics of the event—the *because of* story—would be roughly the same as for the falling brick. But in the case of the falling person we might reasonably expect the full explanation to be more complicated, and we might persist in our inquiry until we discovered *why* the person fell. Was there some telos at work? Some agency? Was suicide the point of the fall? If we determine that the event was purely accidental, then we will be satisfied with the *because of* account, but if we suspect a teleological factor, then we won't rest until we apprehend the meaning of the event in terms of a *so that* account.

Returning now to the circumstances of *der Muselmann*: here we encounter a being for whom there is no *so that* story. *Der Muselmann* is a brick-like entity, a *because of* phenomenon, a mere plaything of environmental forces. We may agree that his heart and kidneys are still functioning *so that* the body will be nourished and purified, but if the whole organism is not engaged by the superordinate telē of an organized personality, then these functions amount to nothing more than residual processes. Such a life—a life without telē—is a life without meaning. If the lesson from *der Muselmann* is that telos is a necessary condition for meaning in life, then our next question must be whether telos is sufficient for meaning.

Consider Sisyphus

Sisyphus is remembered in Greek mythology for being the most deceitful and crafty of mortals. He seduced his niece, usurped his brother's throne, and recklessly exposed the sexual exploits of Zeus. For his hubristic meddling in the affairs of the gods, Sisyphus was condemned to an eternity of tedium and frustration. He was assigned to push a heavy stone up a steep hill, but just as he reached the summit the stone would escape his grasp and roll back to the bottom of the hill, leaving poor Sisyphus to begin again . . . and yet again . . . for eternity.

Unlike *der Muselmann*, Sisyphus has an occupation; his life is *about* something. His telos is to advance the stone to the summit. The point of the story, however, is that a life of tedium and futility, even though it is goal directed, does not constitute a meaningful existence. Indeed, according to the French existentialist philosopher Albert Camus, Sisyphus personifies the utter absurdity of human existence. Just any old purpose, it would appear, is not sufficient to make life meaningful. In order for a telos to confer meaning on a life it must be in some way agreeable to the subject of the life. The life of Sisyphus is not *necessarily* devoid of meaning (since it has a point), but such a life will not be experienced as meaningful unless its activities are satisfying to the subject. In the language of Aristotle we might say that in order for a telos to confer meaning, it must be sufficient to bring the subject to a state of *eudaimonia*, a state of well-being or happiness.

We now have two necessary conditions for judging a life to have meaning: from *der Muselmann* we learn that for one's life to be meaningful there must be some purpose(s) served by the activities of the subject, and from the plight of Sisyphus we learn that the purpose(s) must be sufficient to bring happiness to the subject.

But now we may ask whether satisfying these two necessary conditions is sufficient for a meaningful life. If so, then the life of

Sisyphus would qualify as meaningful only if he could bring himself to enjoy his assignment. If Sisyphus somehow got "into" the job, if he sincerely *wanted* to pursue the cycle of laborious failure, then by these principles we would have to concede that he has a meaningful existence. If it works for Sisyphus, then who are we to judge? There seems to be something commendable in this attitude of tolerance for the pursuits of other persons, yet somehow it doesn't seem quite right. Even if we are willing to grant that Sisyphus leads a subjectively meaningful life there remains the haunting suspicion that it's not deeply meaningful, that his life has meaning merely in some minimal sense. We suspect that it *shouldn't* be meaningful; we suspect that there is something deficient about Sisyphus in his embrace of such a life. Perhaps a less ambiguous example will help.

Consider Villains, Fools, and Derelicts

In *The Brothers Karamazov*, Dostoevsky's Ivan reports on the crimes of Turkish soldiers in Bulgaria:

> They burn villages, murder, outrage women and children, and nail their prisoners by the ears to the fences, leaving them till morning, and in the morning they hang them. . . . These Turks took a pleasure in torturing children too; cutting the unborn child from the mother's womb, and tossing babies up in the air and catching them on the points of their bayonets before their mother's eyes. Doing it before the mother's eyes was what gave zest to the amusement. Here is another scene that I thought very interesting. Imagine a trembling mother with her baby in her arms, a circle of invading Turks around her. They've planned a diversion: they pet the baby to make it laugh. They succeed; the baby laughs. At that moment, a Turk points a pistol four inches from the baby's face. The baby laughs with glee, holds out its little hands to the pistol, and he pulls the trigger in the baby's face and blows out its brains. Artistic, wasn't it?[6]

Most reasonable persons would be loathe to concede that a life in pursuit of such telē could possibly qualify as meaningful. Some ends—subjectively satisfying or not—simply defy justification, and goals that cannot be justified cannot be considered genuinely worthy of pursuit. Now consider the problems raised by individuals who devote their lives to harmless lost causes. Christopher Belshaw asks us to imagine the absurd pursuits of Angelica, the ambitious gardener who busies herself with the task of teaching her flowers to sing.[7] Angelica is invested in a project that she finds worthwhile, and she has a sense of fulfillment, but she is—if anyone is—embarked on a fool's errand. Her pursuit is beyond moral justification for the reason that it violates the first rule of moral discourse: *ought implies can*. That is, it is irrational for anyone to find point in a goal that cannot possibly be accomplished, and those who pursue such goals are fairly accused of engaging in meaningless activities. Happily engaged or not, reason suggests that Angelica's life is devoid of meaning.

To make matters worse, we still have to consider the case of derelicts. Imagine a young woman of immense and varied talents who freely abandons a bright future in favor of life as a bag lady. There she is: on the street living from handout to handout, picking her way through trashcans, while she could be composing operas or saving lives in an operating room somewhere. Her only goal is to survive hour by hour. The moral intuition wants to claim that the young woman's life is meaningless, despite the facts that she harms no one and displays no signs of regret or despair. We feel an urge to say that no one should live such a life, and we are inclined to view her choice as some sort of evidence that she is insane.

Granted, these are extreme examples, but they allow us to see that inserting rational and moral criteria into the equation brings along some serious complications. Just how close is the link between meaning, on one hand, and rational or moral justification, on the other? Our instincts suggest that the lives of villains, fools and derelicts are deficient in meaning because they are deficient in justification. No amount of post hoc rationalization, the gut feels, can make such lives appear meaningful. But how would you react if some self-appointed moralists came along and pronounced your life meaningless because your pursuits failed to measure up to their criteria? The very idea! And yet in the same breath you might yourself declare that poor Angelica is absurdly foolish.

When it comes to our own lives we tend almost exclusively to use the subjective criterion of meaning (happiness), but with respect to others we are quick to apply moral criteria. Obviously, this leaves us with commitments to two different concepts of meaningfulness—one defined by a psychological criterion and the other by a moral criterion. And when we have two concepts trained on the same phenomenon we are likely to generate ambiguity and confusion. This, I believe, is one reason why apprehending the meaning of life has proven to be such an elusive enterprise. And yet we are reluctant to drop either criterion. We expect the psychological and moral criteria to converge, and when they fail to agree—i.e., when happy lives are immoral, or when virtuous lives are unhappy—we are left with a sense that things are out of whack. And if the criteria fail to agree when applied to *our own lives*, then we sense what Thomas Nagel calls the absurd character of human life.[8] Nagel thinks it is a fairly obvious feature of the human condition that we are capable of two modes of judgment about our telē. In the course of everyday life we undertake satisfying goals, and may even succeed in justifying them, thus finding our lives to be meaningful. But then occasionally we are overtaken by self-doubt, when even our most cherished projects appear to have no ultimate point. The universal human capacity to transcend ourselves in reflective thought makes it inevitable that even the most heroic and virtuous lives may be rendered pointless. Sometimes, perhaps when we least expect it, our psychological and moral criteria may fall out of synch, leaving us in a state of bewilderment about the meaning of life.

It is difficult to see where all of this leaves us. Nagel recommends that we simply accept the irony of our dual capacity for committing to telē and doubting our own commitments, and then try not to take ourselves too seriously. He is comfortable with the conclusion that the potential absurdity of the human condition does not necessarily preclude the meaningfulness of human existence. Fits of self-doubt notwithstanding, we have it in our nature to seek goals that we find both personally satisfying and morally defensible. Thus, in addition to the teleological criterion gleaned from *der Muselmann*, and in addition to the psychological criterion gleaned from Sisyphus, we now find good reason to assert that a life cannot be judged meaningful unless it also satisfies a moral criterion. A meaningful life must be morally significant as well as subjectively satisfying; it must be virtuous as well as happy.

Consider the Options

In a formal sense we might declare that our quest to discover the conditions for a meaningful life is now completed: *the meaning of human life consists in the pursuit of goals that enable a marriage of happiness and virtue.* It may be that this general principle for the meaning of life takes us as far as the inquiry can go. Perhaps from here on out it's all up to the individual to find some agenda of projects that happens to be both personally satisfying and morally significant. Finding meaning in life might therefore boil down to something that is theoretically very simple, such as selecting a meal that is both tasty and nutritious. But there is no reason to think that fixing on a general formula for the meaning of life will bring our inquiry to a close. Far from it! For here is where serious inquiry must begin.

Our formula for judging a meaningful life—goals that enable a union of happiness and virtue—may be a lot easier to state than to accomplish. To be sure, many individuals manage to live intensely happy lives. After all, the only requirement for happiness is that we get what we want, and many individuals get just that. Yet such lives are not always meaningful, as Tolstoy's *Confession* attests. Tolstoy had it all—he was wealthy, famous, healthy, well loved by family and friends—and yet he came to a stage in his life when it all felt utterly pointless. He got what everyone wants, but was still left wanting. It is also true that many individuals manage to live consistently virtuous lives that are not in the least happy. What is required for virtue is that we act as we should, and many among us do exactly that. And yet such lives of commendable dutifulness may also be felt to be utterly pointless.

Getting what we want makes us happy, and wanting what is right makes us good, but to achieve happiness and virtue simultaneously is not an easy thing to do. Satisfying our desires often entails a violation of our moral commitments, and honoring our moral commitments often prevents our getting what we want. The secret, of course, is to want only those things that we honestly judge to be good. The most obvious strategy for resolving conflict between desire and virtue would be to conflate the psychological criterion and the moral criterion. That is, one might accept a moral vision as the given and then work on transforming one's desires to come into harmony with objective values. Alternatively, one might accept the subjective factor as fixed and then to bring one's moral vision into line with one's selfish desires. It might be reasoned, for example, that the whole point of moral precepts is to construct a social order in which individuals might maximize their happiness, and if this is the case, then what's wrong with a bit of moral tinkering? If the ultimate point is for the self to love the good, then this might be brought about either by changing the self or changing the good. There may be obvious problems inherent in each of these strategies, but the important thing to see is that it all boils down to the goals that come to be embodied in a life. The challenge in any event is to desire the right goals. Seeking a meaningful life is therefore a quest for moral truth no less than a longing for personal satisfaction.

It is now obvious that we cannot expect to get very far in our inquiry about a meaningful life until we get the question of goals sorted out. Finding the secret to a meaningful life depends, fundamentally, on having a decent theory about the nature of goal seeking, that is, a theory about teleology. What are goals, anyway? What can be said about their reality status? Are they out there somewhere waiting to be discovered, or are they merely invented? What role do goals play in organizing our lives? How do we come to have them? Are they natural, or do they transcend nature? How are goals related to values? How do we judge their merits? What makes achieving them satisfying and worthwhile? If we are seeking some purpose in life, just where and how do we look?

This book takes seriously the idea that the stance we take concerning the nature and dynamics of goals and values will have much to say about how we conduct our individual and collective searches for meaningful lives. What we think about teleology will decisively influence what we are prepared to accept as a union of happiness and virtue. And finding a satisfying way to think about teleology is the challenge of the next two chapters.

PART ONE

THE MEANING OF LIFE

Introduction

The philosophical stakes in the next two chapters run high, for what could be more consequential in a philosophical outlook than the stance it takes on the reality of goals and values? These chapters will ask us to think about the reality of meaning in four different ways:

Meaning is in the world
Meaning is in the mind
Meaning is neither in the world nor in the mind
Meaning is an emergent property

The first three of these options will be covered in chapter 2, and then chapter 3 will focus exclusively on the fourth. The point of these chapters will be to clarify, illustrate, and appraise each of the options. If we can come to a satisfying way to think about teleology, then (in Part Two) we can begin to explore the possibilities for a naturalistic vision of the religious life.

2

The Reality of Meaning

Meaning in the World

Introduction

Our first option for thinking about the nature of goals and values involves the philosophical doctrine known as *realism*. You qualify as a realist about some object of thought, say, a rock, if you believe that the rock really and truly exists out there in the world independently of your thinking about it. The existence of the rock amounts to an objective fact about the extra-mental world, and it is just this fact that makes true your assertion that the rock exists.

Some people—a great many, in fact—take a realist stance on the question of meaning. That is, they believe that in certain important respects the world outside our minds is inherently purposeful. On this view, the world is *about* something, or *for* something. The world is the way it is because it is *meant* to be that way, or it is that way *so that* some definite purpose might be accomplished. There are two different labels that we might attach to this doctrine of meaning. The first is "inherentism," the view that telē are inherent fixtures in the fundamental nature of things, that the world is in some sense constituted by its inherent purpose. The inherentist idea is the same whether the purpose has been imposed on the world from the outside or is naturally endowed with purpose. Goals, functions, designs, ends—these are, according to teleological realists, sewn into the fabric of reality in a fundamental and irreducible way. The other term that might be used for this view is "essentialism." Here the idea is that particular things have the reality and the characteristics they do because they possess a certain identifiable essence. The essence of something tells us what a thing is by definition. It expresses those attributes or functions *without which* the item would not be what it is. For example, an eggbeater that is incapable of beating eggs does not qualify as an eggbeater at all because it fails to perform the essential function of an eggbeater. Or: a figure enclosed by three straight sides does not qualify as a square because it does not satisfy the essential definition of a square. I will be using the less familiar term "inherentism" throughout this book, but in some cases "essentialism" might seem more appropriate.

If, according to inherentism/essentialism, telē are real and essential properties inherent in the extra-mental world, then they might be discovered by inquiry, or perhaps they might be revealed in some way. To achieve a genuinely meaningful life, then, one would first have to apprehend the essential telos (the good) for humanity, and then to transform the self to live in harmony with it. Herein lies the marriage of happiness and virtue.

Inherentism is a very common way to think about how things are in the world. Indeed, it may be the most commonly held metaphysical attitude in human history. Somehow it just seems natural to seek for meaning in the world. The intuitive appeal of inherentism suggests that its deepest origins are psychological rather than historical. The working assumption among most contemporary psychologists is that there is an evolutionary story behind the many neural mechanisms that are involved in producing behavior. The take-home message of this approach to behavior is that the structures of the brain equip humans with something akin to a mental toolkit, that is, a built-in repertoire of behavioral competencies that became part of our biological inheritance because they produced adaptive behaviors in the deep evolutionary past. We arrive in the world all geared up for various reflexes, for particular appetites, for modes of perception, for emotional reactions, for language use, and for patterns of thinking and problem solving.

Some of the most interesting and important modules for mediating behavior are the ones that influence our interactions with other living creatures. Our distant ancestors were preoccupied with food—they needed to find food, of course, but just as importantly they needed to avoid *becoming* food. This means that any chance mutations enhancing their ability to detect predators or prey would have been highly adaptive. Primates that were good at spotting predators and prey had the best chances for surviving and reproducing, whereas their less attentive and discerning competitors died off, leaving no descendants. The eventual result is that natural selection endowed our species with highly sensitive mechanisms for perceiving potential predators and prey. Some investigators have used the term "agent detectors" to describe the neural mechanisms underlying this behavioral competence.[1] So we arrive in the world equipped with agent detectors—both auditory and visual—that are hair-triggered to react with minimal provocation. The slightest movement or noise, or a few fragments hintful of an animate face or body, are likely to produce a judgment that something dangerous or delectable is at hand. The sensitivity of these systems will often result in false positives, that is, beliefs about predators or prey where in fact there are none. This accounts for the tendency of people to see faces in cloud formations and to hear voices whispering in the wind. But when uncertainty prevails and the stakes are high it is better to be safe than sorry. A few mistakes is a small price to pay for high-performance detection systems.

Another impressive item in our mental toolkit is the ability of humans to judge the motives and intentions of fellow humans. In the environment of the Late Pleistocene our most dangerous predators—and our most valued allies—were members of our own species. In these circumstances the ability to guess what other persons were thinking or feeling would have enormous payoffs in terms of predicting how they would behave. Is this person friend or foe? Angry or frightened? Honest or deceitful? The answers could make all the difference between life and death. So in addition to our agent detectors we come equipped with motive detectors, mind-reading modules that inform us quite reliably about the mental states of other persons.

The relevance of these observations to our subject is just this: to a considerable extent the operating systems in our brains are biased to look for meanings in the world. We are wired for making attributions of intention and purpose to the external objects of our experience. We are inclined to make strong inferences about agents and goal-directed behaviors even when the evidence is weak. We instinctively anthropomorphize the inanimate world around us. Consider how we personalize weather systems by naming them, or how we curse at chairs when we stub our toes on them in the dark. And we appear to come to these excesses naturally. There can be little doubt that our brains are biologically prepared to detect purposive phenomena almost everywhere we look. We arrive in the world with teleology on the brain. No wonder, then, that when we seek an understanding of the world around us we intuitively frame our inquiry in terms of *so that* logic. We ask, "*Why* (for what purpose) is there something rather than nothing at all?" A being with teleology on the brain expects to find an answer to this question. Indeed, to such a being, a world without inherent meaning is likely to be experienced as strange, incomplete, and even disconcerting. Encountering such a world might feel a bit like encountering *der Muselmann*.

The point is that we are biased by nature to seek meaning outside ourselves, and then to adjust our agendas accordingly, and we are inclined to this way of thinking without taking prompts from our social environment. But when the social environment happens to provide encouragement and reinforcement along these lines it just makes our unreflective inherentism all the more robust. Social priming heightens preexisting expectations for perceiving purposeful phenomena, increasing the likelihood of making teleological attributions, and once such attributions are made they tend to generate confirming evidence. Inherentism, then, is a persistent metaphysical orientation for two very commanding reasons: first, it is endorsed by our intuitive sense about how things are in the world, and second, it has been actively reinforced by the elaborations of many cultural traditions.

Our inherited mental toolkit may be sufficient for predisposing us to an inherence doctrine of meaning, but unreflective inherentism is not always a stable condition. Consider how two individuals might fall into dispute about whether an object or event has a *so that* story behind it. If Jones thinks that an event was the work of a purposeful agent, but Smith thinks the event happened merely *because of* undirected causes, they might start to give reasons to support their appraisals of the event. If Jones has a compelling argument, then Smith might come around to believing that the event was purposeful, but if Smith prevails then Jones might agree that the event was a mere coincidence. It is not unlikely that this simple dynamic—inquiring skeptics <u>versus</u> apologetic believers—played a role in the development of systematic elaborations of the inherence outlook in the form of religious and philosophical traditions. Here follows an illustrative sampler of such traditions.

Abrahamic Religious Traditions

The three great Abrahamic religions of the world—Judaism, Christianity, Islam—provide us with good examples of the inherentist perspective. Each of these monotheistic traditions is explicit in claiming that the universe was created purposefully by God. This doctrine of providential creation amounts to a pretty large claim, to be sure. If God created the universe, then it may be said that God serves as the ultimate explanation for everything that happens in the universe. And if the universe was created for divine purposes, then it may also be said that those purposes serve as the ultimate justification for everything that happens. Moreover, the claim implies that every entity and event in the history of the universe has some point, some significance, relative to God's purposes in creation. The Abrahamic traditions may not always be in clear agreement about what the divine purposes are, or the extent to which they might be known, but they have never wavered in the assertion that the world exists *because of* God's creative act, and *so that* God's purposes might be realized. To the Abrahamic mind neither the external world of things nor the internal world of experience can be understood or tolerated apart from the inherent telē ordained by God.

The Abrahamic traditions have consistently maintained that human beings have a unique place in God's creation. Like everything else in the universe humans were created for a purpose, but they bear a special relationship to God and have therefore been assigned a special purpose. Humans are presumed to be like God in ways that other creatures are not. Like God, humans are free agents, an essential attribute that distinguishes them from all other creatures. As free agents, humans have creative powers and the capacity for justice and mercy, but they can also choose to be destructive, unjust, and merciless. Rather than saying humans are *like God*, the traditions tell us that humans were created *to be* like God, or *meant* to be Godlike. This reading makes it clear that humans were created *for* something, they were created with an assigned telos.

The inherentism of the Abrahamic traditions is unmistakable: the world, specifically humankind, was purposefully created as an instrument for executing God's will. The cosmos is intended; it is a moral order infused with objective values. Humans are meant to serve God, to be divinely appointed agents, so any human actions that are not in keeping with this assigned telos are clearly misdirected and ultimately meaningless. According to Abrahamic traditions, serving God's will is a necessary condition for a meaningful life. While serving God may be virtuous, it is also possible to serve God begrudgingly and unhappily. But as we have seen, no life can be judged meaningful if it does not represent a union of both happiness and virtue. Serving God is sufficient for happiness only if one genuinely *desires* to serve God. And here we encounter the central challenge faced by all the Abrahamic traditions: the challenge of self-transformation. In order for a person to desire serving God's will, it is necessary that the person displace his or her agenda and embrace instead God's agenda. The person must give up self-interest and willfully submit to a condition of slavery to God's will. The marriage of happiness and virtue is captured in these words from the Hebrew Psalmist: "With my mouth open I pant, because I long for your commandments" (Ps. 119:131).

The Socratic School of Philosophy

The philosophers of the Socratic school (Socrates, Plato, Aristotle) gave systematic formulation to the inherence doctrine in response to the radical skepticism of their Sophist rivals. The main tenets of the Socratic school were, contra Sophism, that truth and value were objectively real and that they were accessible to rational inquiry. Plato and Aristotle were anxious to demonstrate that certain telē—traditional moral and political ends—were actually grounded in the fundamental nature of reality and were discoverable by reason. Plato's metaphysical version of inherentism was sharply dualistic. He believed that the material objects of everyday experience were endowed with essences by virtue of their being particular manifestations of universal and transcendent forms. Plato describes the soul as having three parts—the rational, the spirited and the appetitive—with each part having an essential function. The telos of the rational soul is to come to know truth and goodness by rational means, and then to discipline the spirited and appetitive parts of the soul, directing them to love, and thereby to serve, the eternal good. The union of happiness and virtue is achieved in the harmonization of the soul.

Aristotle agreed with Plato on the basic Socratic principles, but he had different ideas about how to proceed philosophically. He rejected Plato's dualism, placing form and matter in a single metaphysical domain, united under the concept of substance. A substance is an item of *formed matter*. The Parthenon, for example, is a substance: it has properties of *this-ness* (matter) and *what-ness* (form). For Aristotle, something is real if and only if it possesses the contingent properties of matter in union with the necessary (essential) properties of form. Whereas Plato took permanence to be the salient feature to be explained by philosophy, Aristotle regarded change as the central object of inquiry. He was impressed by the fact that substances are constantly changing their form. Motion, generation, growth, decay— such changes are going on around us all the time. To understand the world, Aristotle thought, was to understand the dynamics of change.

In Aristotle's view all changes in substances were to be construed in terms of a transition from potentiality to actuality of form. For example, the universal form, or essence, of "oak tree" is inherent in the acorn, but in a state of potentiality. We can see Aristotle's inherentism in his view that each substance contains within itself a teleological principle that guides the process of change. That is, each substance possesses a self-contained *entelechy* (literally: inherent telos). The entelechy of a substance is a principle of causation, for it explains why acorns become oak trees rather than, say, leopards. But there is more to the story of causation than this. Aristotle recognized four types of cause, all acting in concert. When we observe a change in some substance, X, we may ask the following questions:

1. What is X made of? (the material cause; *this-ness*)

2. What is X made into? (the formal cause; *what-ness*)

3. What are the means of change? (the efficient cause; *how* the change occurred)

4. What is the point of change? (the final cause, telos; *why* the change occurred)

No change, Aristotle insisted, is fully intelligible until we have complete answers to all four questions (in natural changes the answers to numbers 2 and 4 are identical, but in artificial changes they are different).

More than anything else, Aristotle wanted to know what humans are for. That humans are for something follows from the general principle that every substance (including every person) is by nature aimed toward the good of its kind. This is the starting point for Aristotle's *Nicomachean Ethics*, where his views on the meaning of life are systematically developed in a grand vision of the union of happiness and virtue. The following series of questions and answers attempts to capture the main ideas of the book.

Q: What is the point of any art, inquiry, action or pursuit?
A: Each of these aims to some good.

Q: What, then, is good?
A: The greatest good is happiness (eudaimonia).

Q: What, then, is happiness?
A: Happiness is the state of living well and doing well.

Q: How can we live well and do well (i.e., be happy)?
A: By making proper choices.

Q: How do we know what proper choices are?
A: Proper choices are those that serve to actualize the inherent telos (entelechy) of a substance.

Q: What, then, is the human entelechy?
A: Virtue.

Q: What, then, is virtue?
A: Virtues are either practical or contemplative.

Q: What are practical virtues?
A: Habits of action formed in accordance with right reason.

Q: What, then, is right reason?
A: Whatever advances, and does not disrupt, proper functioning.

Q: What disrupts proper functioning?
A: Excesses or defects of passion.

Q: How does right reason avoid these?
A: By controlling the passions and choosing the mean between excess and defect.

Q: What are some examples of practical virtue?
A: Courage, temperance, pride, generosity, justice.

Q: What is the point of living in the mean between excesses and defects?
A: Living in the mean frees the soul to pursue contemplative virtue.

Q: What, then, is contemplative virtue?
A: Wisdom, that being the rational state of mind that possesses invariable truths about first principles.

Q: What is the point of achieving contemplative virtue?
A: Wisdom is the ultimate point, the greatest good; it is the actualization of human potential for reason.

Q: But originally, wasn't happiness said to be the greatest good?
A: (in Aristotle's own words): "What is by nature proper to each thing will be at once the best and the most pleasant for it. In other words, a life guided by intelligence is the best and most pleasant for man, inasmuch as intelligence, above all else, is man. Consequently, this kind of life is the happiest."[2]

Modern Philosophy

Even though there had been occasional doubts raised about particular versions of inherentism over the centuries, the general perspective itself was not seriously challenged from the time of Aristotle until the seventeenth century CE. In some respects the intellectual history of the ancient and medieval periods may be read as a sustained and successful attempt to keep the inherence doctrine of meaning intact. But despite its intuitive advantage, and despite centuries' worth of rigorous care and feeding, the presumption of inherentism could not easily withstand the challenge generated by the rise of modern science.

Among the most radical changes attending the rise of modern science was a decisive shift in what counted as a genuine explanation. Medieval scholasticism had left the Aristotelian quartet of causes intact, but by far the most important of these was final causation, the teleological explanation. The medieval mind found *because of* explanations (efficient causes) to be less interesting and satisfying than *so that* explanations (final causes). Indeed, efficient causal explanations were not sought for their own sake, but mostly for their role in calling attention to final causal explanations. *How* God brought about events in the world was of little consequence in comparison with *why* events took place. The gold standard for explanation throughout the medieval period was teleological. Gradually, however, the burden of explanation shifted in favor of efficient and material causes.

Johannes Kepler, Galileo Galilei and Francis Bacon—almost exact contemporaries of the late sixteenth and early seventeenth centuries—had become impassioned advocates for the view that the universe was a massive project in applied geometry, a complex and beautiful system of mathematical harmonies. They believed that God had written the book of nature in the language of mathematics, and the way to understand the phenomena of nature was to quantify them. The new standard of explanation was worked out by giving precise meanings to previously vague notions, such as force, resistance, velocity, acceleration, space, and time. The idea was to ignore extraneous considerations, such as Aristotle's final causes, and to concentrate on isolating variables, assigning mathematical values to them, and identifying invariant relations between them.

For these early scientists, then, things happen in nature, not *so that* inherent potentials might be actualized, but rather *because of* fixed and unvarying mathematical relations. If anything is inherent in the world it is these universal mathematical harmonies, not goals or purposes. If theologians wish to speak of inherent telē, then let them, but the business of science is to traffic in the efficient causes that regulate matter. The upshot of this shift in explanation was that the quantifiable properties of matter were taken by the new science as the true measure of reality. If a putative property could not be measured in any way, then how can we say it is really there? When we add to this picture a growing acceptance of the corpuscular (atomic) theory of matter, we get a clear sense of the brave new world that was opened up by modern science. The physical universe was a realm of material bodies in motion, governed by blind mechanical forces. The anthropocentric and teleological guts of the ancient and medieval world pictures were simply factored out. *Because of* explanations were quite enough to make the world intelligible. There might well be a personal creator and divine purposes at work far behind the scenes, but to the eye of a dispassionate observer equipped with the methods and assumptions of the new science, there appeared nothing but atoms forced to move in space and time, wherein objects of sense behaved according to fixed laws. Entities appeared and events took place *because of* these laws, not *so that* anything.

Initially, the early modern scientists factored out the role of teleological causation by simply ignoring it. The idea was that genuinely purposeful phenomena might exist, but they were not relevant to the task of comprehending the natural world. It was not long, however, before the concept of teleology was explicitly rejected—it was not that telē were irrelevant, but that they simply did not exist. An important ingredient in this movement from ignoring the causal role of purpose to rejecting the reality of purpose altogether was the resurrection of an ancient distinction between primary and secondary qualities. The ancient philosopher, Democritus, was the first to bring this distinction to light, but once it was rediscovered during the Renaissance it became a central feature of the modern scientific worldview, having devastating consequences for the inherentist doctrine.

The primary qualities were thought to be fundamental properties inherent in matter. These qualities—size, shape, motion, number, solidity—were quantifiable properties, the true and proper subject matter for science. The secondary qualities—color, taste, smell, sound, warmth—might be undeniable aspects of experience, but these qualities did not appear to correspond to anything in the material world. When, for example, you perceive the shape of an object it was supposed that this subjective quality corresponds one-to-one to an actual physical property in the extra-mental world. But when you perceive an object to be warm or colorful the story is different. These subjective qualities do not correspond to physical qualities in the same direct way. The experience of shape is caused by actual shapes in the world, but the experience of warmth is not caused by actual warmth, it is caused by minute details persisting among primary qualities. Seeing the color of a red apple does not mean that the apple itself is red (it isn't), but rather means that the apple has a peculiar surface texture (minute shapes) that absorbs some light frequencies and reflects others, creating the illusion that redness is inherent in the extra-mental world. Secondary qualities are then merely derivations of the more basically real primary qualities of things. In other words, the reality of secondary qualities reduces to the reality of primary qualities. Color, taste, smell, sound, and warmth may exist in experience, but they do not exist in the world.

While this distinction between primary and secondary qualities was accepted by all the major players during the rise of modern science, it would be misleading to suggest that it was given a common metaphysical interpretation, which it wasn't. But it was increasingly evident that the world of subjective experience was becoming a repository for all those pesky phenomena that could not be formulated by the new science. And this was precisely the fate of teleological phenomena. Telē were banished—along with color, warmth, and smell—to the domain of the mind.

Keenly aware of the impact that the new science was having on traditional values, René Descartes took philosophical measures that would simultaneously protect the autonomy of science and reinforce the integrity of the inherence doctrine of meaning. He reinstated inherentism by revitalizing Plato's metaphysical dualism. The fundamental Cartesian distinction was between material substance (the essential attribute of which was *extension*), and mental substance (with *thought* as the essential attribute). The primary qualities (size, shape, etc.) pertained to material substance, while the secondary qualities (color, taste, etc.) qualified mental substance. The inherentist doctrine was preserved because telē were inherent in mental substance, and mental substance was just as fundamentally real as material substance, both having been created by God.

Descartes believed that the defining essence of humanity was radical freedom. Nonhuman animals were mere mechanisms, entirely governed by the physical laws of nature. But humans were created by God to be Godlike, and this means that nothing governs the human will but the will itself. For Descartes the only condition for a meaningful life is to choose freely to let the will be governed by reason alone in all its particular choices. If the will remains in a perpetual state of submission to reason, and then follows rational choices with firm resolve, the meaningful life will follow. Descartes' vision of the moral life is very Aristotelian: ultimately, there can be no conflict between happiness and virtue, for both are to be achieved simultaneously by the rational exercise of human freedom.

From the time of Descartes right through to the end of the Enlightenment, moral philosophy was dominated by rationalism. The central idea was that both the physical world and the life of the mind were governed by rational principles. The rational principles governing the physical world are discoverable by natural science, resulting in the formulation of natural laws. It was widely presumed that there existed a set of moral rules analogous to the laws of nature, and these too were discoverable by the moral equivalent to natural science. The result of this rational inquiry would be a detailed formulation of universal moral law. Descartes himself never realized this ideal, but he made an interesting beginning. In large measure, the history of moral philosophy during the modern period may be read as a sustained attempt to complete the project. Those who disparaged the project generally came to believe that genuine meaning is to be found neither in the world nor in the mind (and for samples of this way of thinking we shall have to wait).

Process Philosophy

At the risk of exceeding the scope of this book I will include one final (contemporary) example of the inherence perspective: the process philosophy of Alfred North Whitehead. Process philosophy may be seen as an attempt to render inherentism compatible with the revolutionary developments in early-twentieth-century physics. As noted, early modern science initially ignored, and then deplored, teleological explanations in favor of *because of* explanations. Whitehead developed a nondualistic way of thinking that put telē back into the fundamental fabric of the world.

Following the lead of Leibniz, Whitehead rejected the metaphysics of substance (whether material, mental, or both), preferring instead to develop a metaphysics of process. He felt obliged in this direction because relativity and quantum theory were presenting us with a view that the ultimate constituents of reality "happen" rather than "endure"; the world is an active field of momentary and overlapping *events*, not a geometrical arrangement of durable and passive *things*.[4] Whitehead also felt compelled to characterize the constituents of reality in terms of experience (though not necessarily conscious experience, which he considered to be a rare thing in the world). He felt so compelled because he could not imagine how the undeniably real qualities of experience could possibly derive from nonexperiential constituents. Here we are able to see why Whitehead took such a dim view of the world picture presented by modern science: he found it completely lacking in the conceptual resources required to render an account of experience. How might a pile of experienceless atoms ever come to generate experiencing brains? If experiences are real, which they undeniably are, then there should be a satisfying answer. But modern philosophy offered none. This question, incidentally, is what contemporary philosophers of mind refer to as "the hard problem."

Whiteheadian metaphysics, then, envisions a world that comes fleeting into (and out of) existence as a result of countless bursts of experience. Here's a fanciful way to think about this. Imagine yourself looking out over a meadow where billions of fireflies are milling about. Now imagine that the fireflies get themselves organized and simultaneously light up in a particular configuration. You just might get to see an elephant strolling across the meadow. Such entities, we say, become "objectified" as a consequence of fireflies flashing, but this is precisely the way that things become objectified (on Whitehead's account) when occasions of experience become actualized. It was Whitehead's view that the energetic phenomena explored by physics *just are* these occasions of experience. To see how teleology is brought into this picture we need to look more closely at the internal dynamics of these occasions.

In Whitehead's cosmology all causation is located in the input-output dynamics of momentary experiences (occasions), a kind of respiratory function by which occasions become objectified. If nothing happens there then nothing happens anywhere. These momentary events constitute the link between past and future. Between its initial inputs from the past and its culminating output to the future each occasion is characterized by a unique subjective immediacy, a very brief lifespan of enjoyment. Ultimately, what happens during this lifetime is a process of evaluation and choice. During the input phase the occasion receives influences from the entire past history of the entire cosmos (sounds strange, I know). Everything that happens, everywhere, comes to bear upon the unfolding event. This is the *given* to which the occasion is called to respond, and in the process of response each occasion becomes an objectified influence on future events everywhere in the cosmos. The response of each occasion to its past is constrained by the events of the past (which keeps the cosmos orderly), but it is not absolutely determined by them (which allows for novelty in cosmic history). The input phase also includes the endowment of an initial aim, or purpose (entelechy?) provided by God. The given that each occasion has to work with, therefore, amounts to all the facts of cosmic history plus one aim, or value, representing God's will for the occasion's final act of self-creation. The initial aim represents the inherent good for the occasion, what it *ought* to do from God's perspective.

God's role in this process is roughly the same as the role played by each unfolding occasion. God "reads in" the state of the creation at every instant and then determines what the ideal initial aim should be for every single emerging occasion. God makes these determinations for the sake of cosmic harmony. It's as if God hands out unique work orders to each momentary occasion, such that the work order specifies the ideal purpose, the objective meaning, for each occasion's existence. If each occasion followed the initial aim provided by God, then the state of the cosmos in its next moment would be one of maximum possible harmony for that moment (given the possibilities laid down by the facts of the past).

But of course it doesn't always happen that occasions do as they should. The initial aim gets modified in the course of an occasion's subjective assessment process, and thus there may arise a discrepancy between what an occasion *should* do (initial aim) and what an occasion *desires* to do (modified aim). This discrepancy is possible because it is in the nature of occasions that they are drawn to maximize the intensity of their own satisfaction, for their own sake. The final task for an emerging occasion, then, is to make a choice that resolves the tension between two values: the objective value inherent in God's provision of an initial aim, and the subjective value inherent in the occasion's natural inclination for self-enjoyment. Only God can determine what is best for the world at large (virtue), and only the occasion, given its unique perspective, can determine what is best for itself (happiness). It would appear, then, that every occasion amounts to a meaningful event, more or less, depending on the extent to which the occasion conforms to the objective value of the God-given initial aim.

The issue at stake in Part One of this book is whether or not there exist any objectively real telē—goals, values, purposes—that can tell us what human beings are *for*. I have suggested that we are left with four ways to answer this question. The first option, inherent-ism, claims that there are such telē, and that these are embedded in the fundamental nature of the real world, there to be apprehended by inquiry or revelation. As we shall see, inherentism has drawn its share of criticism over the centuries, and it has now become difficult to see how the more robust forms of this perspective (sampled above) can be given plausible defense.

Meaning in the Mind

Introduction

Our mental toolkit appears to bias us toward the inherentist presumption that values are established in the world in the way facts are. Facts are just what they are, regardless of what anyone thinks about them. They are the extra-mental realities that make our beliefs true or false. Inherentism wants us to treat values in the same way, namely, as extra-mental realities that make our actions right or wrong, regardless of our thinking. Facts and values, on this view, do the same kind of work because they belong to the same species. But there appear to be several perfectly sound reasons to challenge this inherentist presumption. For one thing, it seems quite odd to say that values are what they are *despite* our thinking about them, whereas it seems quite natural to say that values are what they are precisely *because* of the way we think about them. And if this is right, then the truth question will play out differently. Factual claims, we might agree, are judged true or false relative to the way the external (objective) world is constituted, but value claims are judged true or false relative to the way the internal (subjective) world is constituted.

Thus we are brought to a second way to think about our subject: meaning is in the mind. There are several possible labels for this view—"relativism," "perspectivism," constructivism," "inventionism," "postmodernism"—but in any case the principle is the same: the reality of values is grounded in psychological and social contingencies, not in metaphysical absolutes. I will use the less familiar term *inventionism* to carry the burden of this section.

Inventionists typically, though not exclusively, share a deep suspicion of metaphysical speculation. Those who do engage in metaphysics normally end up as dualists or idealists, but for most inventionists the important questions are fixed on the knower rather than the known, epistemology rather than metaphysics. Inventionists are drawn to the particular rather than the universal, a bias that naturally tends toward skepticism about dogmatic notions involving "the essential human condition" or "the universal meaning of life." Such notions are deserving candidates for debunking, a service inventionists are only too eager to provide.

Consider, for example, how quickly the inherentism of the Abrahamic traditions dissolves into contingency. It is easy to say that the universal meaning of human life is to serve God's will, but when it comes to figuring out what God's will *is* things get complicated. The sources for discerning the will of God are plural, often obscure or ambiguous, and more than occasionally conflicting. What this means is that anyone motivated to serve God's will must engage in the appraisal and interpretation of multiple sources, and here is where inherentism begins to falter. Unavoidably, the only way to "discover" God's will is to sort through a thicket of diverse possibilities and to make subjective decisions about meaning. God's will concerning a particular set of options for one's life may be construed in radically diverse ways (how often has the same God of Abraham been allied to opposing forces in war?). So when you come right down to particulars, God's will can be made to come out in any way imaginable, which is to say that God's will effectively amounts to whatever individuals or groups imagine it to be. And if this is the case, then it begins to look as if the meaning of life is less to be discovered in the world than it is to be constructed in the mind.

For inventionists, human reality is too complex, too variable, and too contextual to be summed up in convenient inherentist categories. It is not that inventionists disparage the quest for meaning—indeed, they relish it—or claim that there are no morally defensible telē, but rather that these matters cannot be worked out in isolation from the concrete and variable circumstances in which individuals and groups find themselves. Telē are not ahistorical, they are not context-neutral, and they are definitely not extra-mental. If, according to inventionists, there are no teleological imperatives scripted into the cosmos, or issued by divine oracles, or self-evident to reasoned reflection, then the holy grail of uniting happiness and virtue must be constructed by the subjective imagination, or negotiated by social interaction.

And now for another sampling . . .

Sophists

Early in the fifth century BCE, Athens became a cauldron of intellectual controversy: the Sophists had arrived. The Sophists were a disparate group of itinerant teachers, moving from place to place providing lessons in rhetoric and the practical arts of living to affluent young patrons. They were enlightened cosmopolitans who had traveled extensively and possessed encyclopedic knowledge of the laws and customs of diverse cultures. They caused intellectual upheaval because they promoted a doctrine of cultural relativism, forcing young Athenians to consider whether the ideas and customs of their tradition represented the rock of truth or merely a tissue of convention. For their part, the Sophists were deeply skeptical: what we call truth, they insisted, was really just expediency and habit, having no moorings in the fundamental nature of things.

Athens was ripe for such views. The presocratic tradition of philosophy, from Thales onward, had amounted to an adventure in speculative cosmology, that is, setting down the ultimate physical truths about the cosmos. This tradition had produced a confusing array of world pictures, but no consensus. Thales taught that the original substance of all reality was *water*; Anaximander said the original stuff was the invisible and boundless *apeiron*; Anaximenes put it out that the essential ingredient of reality was *air*, Empedocles upped the stakes to four essential substances (air, earth, fire, water); Heraclitus insisted that the salient features of reality were diversity and flux, while Parmenides said reality was an indivisible and immutable Unity. Such a diversity of competing claims eroded confidence in the distinction between true knowledge and mere opinion. The Sophists turned the heads of young Athenians away from this tradition of speculative cosmology to concentrate on the relativity of the human condition, thereby deepening the crisis of intellectual confidence.

The Sophists were pragmatic, emphasizing the practical necessity of making a living in a competitive environment. They claimed "virtue" as their subject matter, by which they meant the art of rhetorical manipulation. To thrive in the dog-eat-dog political ecology of Athens one needed the power of persuasion to bring circumstances to one's own advantage. Virtue, for the Sophists, amounted to the power to succeed.

Protagoras, the most famous of the Athenian Sophists, used analogies to perception in demonstrating the relativity of human knowledge. Two persons viewing the same object will of necessity have different things to say about it because their positions relative to the object are different. Likewise, two persons feeling the same breeze will have different impressions of its warmth. In these cases, who can claim to give the correct description of the object, and who can say whether the breeze itself is warm or cold? Truth, therefore, is relative to the subject, which seems to be the thrust of Protagoras's famous statement that "man is the measure of all things." The same lesson applies to moral judgments. Protagoras denied that inquiry might bring us to discover universal laws of right conduct. Every society invents its own laws to address its own needs, and fixes them by convention, not by extracting them from the order of nature or by listening to the gods.

For Protagoras, virtue was construed in a surprisingly conservative manner. He advised that the relativity of moral values did not legitimate wanton selfishness or hedonism. Instead, individuals should respect the established ethos of their own society because at the end of the day—all things being relative—this ethos is bound to be as good as any other, and conforming to it has the advantage of maintaining the continuity of civil order that is requisite for any measure of happiness. The radical Sophist, Thrasymachus, took the relativist doctrine in a different direction. In his view, "man the measure" amounts to "might makes right." We should not feel obliged to conform to conventional conceptions of justice, he said, for these conceptions are instruments of oppression, invented by the ruling party to advance and preserve their own interests. Just laws are not scripted into the cosmos or disclosed by the gods; they are merely reflections of self-interest and must be opposed by self-interest. As we have seen, these inventionist principles advanced by the Sophists were the occasion for an inherentist reaction developed by the Socratic school.

Existentialism

The general mood of the Enlightenment was one of cheery confidence in reason. The emergence of the new science had delivered Europe from a long dark period of superstition, bringing with it the revelation that nature was a deeply rational order. Renaissance scholars and early modern philosophers (Descartes, Spinoza, Leibniz) had brought forward the influence of Stoicism, one of the brightest lights of the Enlightenment. Stoic doctrine was inherentist: it held that the wise person always lives in harmony with nature, and since nature is governed by inherent reason (logos), it follows that the ultimate telos for humanity is to live by the dictates of reason. This ethos of Stoic inherentism dominated moral theory from the time of Montaigne and Descartes to the close of the Enlightenment, fueling the optimistic notion that intellectual and social progress would continue unabated so long as humans followed the course of reason.

Cheery confidence about the fruits of reason began to wane, however, in the closing decades of the eighteenth century. For many, the horrors of the French Revolution dispelled the optimistic notion that humans were essentially rational creatures. Hume's skeptical critique of human understanding devastated confidence in the power of rational inquiry, and the misery attending the industrial revolution challenged uncritical belief in progress. The sense of blessed harmony with nature was being disrupted by a sense of alienation and loss of control. The Apollonian detachment and restraint of the Enlightenment were about to give way to a Dionysian upsurge of engagement and spontaneity.

Critics of the Enlightenment were not satisfied with the place it assigned to humanity. It is one thing to characterize the physical universe as a vast machine rigidly obeying the eternal laws of the natural order, but it is quite another to conclude that the ultimate telos for humanity is to mimic this mechanism by conforming to narrow constraints on ambition and expression. The Enlightenment picture of human reality was just too simplistic. Humans are not essentially detached and dispassionate cognitive machines, they are not essentially reducible to rational formulae, and they are not mere objects or abstractions. Rather, human beings are concrete subjects, passionately engaged in the messy particulars of an unruly world that is frequently at odds with their deepest longings. The inventionist thinking of existentialism set out to show that human existence is more than the Enlightenment version of Stoic inherentism made it out to be.

Søren Kierkegaard grew up in Copenhagen during a time when the Danish church had succumbed to Enlightenment religion, a cozy blend of Christianity and Stoicism. The sermons he heard as a young man resembled lectures—arid, intellectual, and absolutely uninspiring. Kierkegaard's own understanding of Christianity had convinced him that the ideals of the Enlightenment had distorted Christianity beyond recognition. According to Enlightenment religion, an individual should always believe and act in conformity with reason, rational inquiry being our most reliable guide. But Kierkegaard was convinced that inquiry was never enough to bring us to choose as we must. Achieving the greatest good is less a matter of the intellect than it is a matter of the will. He insisted that the ultimate telos for humankind was the life of faith, and rational inquiry can never bring us to faith. At best, reason can support the approximate truth of Christianity, but Kierkegaard's Christianity requires more than a lukewarm approximate response; it requires complete submission. We are called, Kierkegaard thought, to perform a "teleological suspension of the ethical," that is, the religious response must be made in violation of rational moral dictates. This, he thought, was well illustrated in the biblical story of Abraham and Isaac. Abraham is commanded by God to sacrifice his only son, Isaac. But this action would be, by all rational standards of moral behavior, completely absurd. And yet Abraham, as a man of faith, must obey God's will—to fulfill his telos he was compelled to suspend rational judgment.[5]

The life of faith, for Kierkegaard, was the only genuinely meaningful life, representing the highest virtue and promising the greatest happiness. But it was not a life that one could achieve by following the dictates of reason. Faith was, by all rational standards, objectively false. Kierkegaard asks his readers to decide which quest has the most truth: the dispassionate observer who inquires about God objectively, or the passionate seeker who is driven by ultimate concern to enter a relationship with God? His answer is that anyone who prefers the objective mode has been corrupted by science. This sharp contrast between subjective and objective modes led Kierkegaard to claim that "truth is subjectivity." Enlightenment thinkers glorified objectivity, impartiality and detachment, but this mode of being was anathema to Kierkegaard. Indeed, such a stance would amount to an impossible, deeply false existence. The idea that religious truth, or any truth, is independent of how one thinks about it was inconceivable to Kierkegaard. Disinterested truth is a sorry contradiction. Meaning, telos—if there is any such thing—*must* be subjective. If this looks objectively absurd, then so much the better.[6]

Friedrich Nietzsche lived during the second half of the nineteenth century, a time when the effects of industrialization and urbanization were getting ugly. The feeling of many was that human life was becoming commercialized and vulgar, and there was a growing sense of anonymity, isolation, alienation, and dehumanization. Nietzsche's driving concern in such a world centered on the question of human meaning: How does one find telos in a world that is nihilistic, irrational, impersonal, and Godless? Finding a way of life is not a fitting subject for rational inquiry, however, because ways of life are far too complicated and fluid to submit to demonstration. A meaningful life must be an original work of art.

Nietzsche agreed with Kierkegaard's view that disinterested thought was an absurdity. There is no such thing as "pure" reason or "timeless" knowledge. All thought, all inquiry, is relative to time and circumstance; all "truths" are contingent interpretations; all knowing is *active* and ultimately autobiographical. Nietzsche mirrors the perspective of the Sophists: where you stand—your beliefs, desires, memories, fears—determines what you see and how you think. He was highly critical of the childish manner in which philosophers spin out claims to universal and timeless truths. Every great philosophy, he thought, amounts to little more than a confession of personal biases. Objective truth and meaning are fictions, passing fancies of interpretation.

How, then, does one become a genuine human being in a dehumanizing world where none of the answers to the abyss of life transcend the interests of those who give them? Nietzsche's answer to this question is given in his concept of "will to power," which is probably best construed as "creativity." Nietzsche was impressed by those individuals who were able to look into the abyss of life and still have the courage to create something original—individuals who had the fortitude and self-mastery to sweep aside received "truths" and to construct their own creative interpretations. He agreed with Kierkegaard that to find genuine meaning in life one had to be exceptional, extraordinary, original. Nietzsche deeply admired the artistic spirit, which is often irreverent and violent, but most notably driven by intense passion for self-invention.

For Jean-Paul Sartre the beginning point for philosophy is the fact that God does not exist. The disturbing thing about this fact is that it leaves us in a state of anxious confusion about what human existence is *for*. As long as God was on the scene we had the assurance that we were designed by God to serve a purpose, we had an essence, an assigned telos. But if there is no God who made us, then human life has all the marks of randomness and absurdity. A nauseating thought.

The loss of God, Sartre thinks, forces us to come to terms with the idea that there is no such thing as human nature. He expresses this idea in the central doctrine of existentialism: *existence precedes essence.*[7] What this means is that humans are nothing (no essence, no *whatness*) until they first exist. That is, there is no way to tell what human beings will be like, what they will do, in advance of their existing. The same cannot be said of any other entities in the universe. We know what frogs and mice and lamps will be like in advance of their existence. For such entities the proper formula is *essence precedes existence*. Before a lamp can exist, its nature must be conceived in the mind of the lampsmith. Mice and frogs are only slightly different: we know in advance what they will be like because they are so tightly constrained by their genetic makeup that their lives are predictable. When you've seen one frog you've seen them all, and you know what to expect of the next one even before it exists. Humans, however, lack such constraints. Humans are radically free to be any number of things, and there's no way of telling how things will go.

Humans are thrown into the world with no telos but to invent one. To be a human being is like being called up out of the blue and offered a job. Your obvious first response would be to ask what sort of job it is. But how would things look if the caller replied, "Hey, it's *your job*, you tell *me*"? Humans are thrown into the world without being intended *for* anything at all, but they become what they will be by making free choices. At first we are nothing, but by our own invention we become something. Our *thisness* becomes a *whatness*, not by working out an inherent telos, but by inventing a telos to be worked out. We are for whatever we decide to be for.

For Sartre, human beings are "condemned to be free"—free because we have no preassigned purpose, and condemned because this condition is anxiety-producing. "What if we get it wrong?" one might ask. But this would be a silly question because if there is no preassigned point to human existence, then there's no right or wrong way to get it. This implies, of course, that conventional moral theory is out of the question. If there are no objective standards for judging goals and actions right or wrong, then there can be no substantial moral philosophy. In response to this important charge, Sartre offers a distinction between formal and material moral judgments. He admits that material moral judgments are unwarranted—for example, I cannot justify criticizing you for choosing to torture animals. But there are grounds for judging the *form* of one's moral choices. If you run away from your responsibility for inventing yourself (say, by falling victim to peer pressure), then Sartre would accuse you of being *inauthentic* (i.e., not authoring yourself). To live by the telē assigned to you by others is to relinquish your freedom, and that would be to live as a mere object, not a free agent. To live the authentic life, Sartre suggests, requires the courage to act freely and the integrity to accept, without excuses, responsibility for one's actions.

Postmodernism

Postmodernism amounts to a full-scale critique and rejection of the intellectual moorings set down during the Enlightenment. Enlightenment mentality was obsessed with a concern for certainty, and satisfied this urge by constructing metaphysical, epistemological, and moral foundations, including the metaphysical concept of substance (material, mental, and divine), epistemological notions of clarity and distinctness (innate ideas, sense data), and universal moral principles (pleasure, liberty). These foundations were all established, of course, on the claim that they represented the objective dictates of reason.

Postmodernists did not originate the critique of these foundations—the basics are all there in Hume, Kant, and Nietzsche—but they did intensify and diversify the critique.

Here's a simplified way to characterize the postmodern spirit: if you politicize Nietzsche and amplify the results, then you get postmodernism. The radical perspectivism of the existentialist movement centered on the autonomy of the individual, but the postmodern critique tends to reduce the subject to networks of social relations, leaving political entities at the center of analysis. Whereas existentialism locates meaning in the subject, postmodernism finds it in groups. Existentialists invent meaning by creative imagination, but postmodernists do it by social negotiation. Nietzsche found a multiplicity of interpretations at the level of biography, while postmodernism finds the multiplicity at the level of ethnography. The postmodern project also broadens the Nietzschean initiative to include critiques of all cultural forms, including literature, art, politics, science, technology, and religion.

The Enlightenment ideal was to construct a comprehensive and final set of ideas that that would unify our beliefs about truth and goodness in such a way that personal aspirations for happiness might be harmonized with public norms of virtue. Richard Rorty, an important source of inspiration for postmodernism, challenges the idea that a final vocabulary about anything at all can be established, let alone one that attempts to integrate ideas about truth with ideas about justice. He does not denigrate efforts to formulate perspectives on the order of nature (though he dismisses claims of their objectivity and finality), and he does not disparage attempts to formulate individual and collective telē (though he dismisses attempts to justify them by extra-mental standards). What he objects to, most fundamentally, is the philosophical aspiration—a pipedream—to make these cohere in a single vocabulary. Rorty goes farther to reject attempts to unify the goal of self-creation with the goal of social solidarity, goals that he finds equally valid but deeply incommensurate: "There is no way to bring self-creation together with justice at the level of theory."[8] In other words, therapy and politics may each be worthy undertakings, but they constitute radically different language games. The self is contingent and communities are contingent, but their contingency is relative to different dynamics. We can never transcend the contingency of the self in a way that might generate a universal conception of human nature. Sorry, but the marriage of happiness and virtue is on the rocks from the start.

Rorty thinks we are simply deluded if we presume, as philosophers are eager to do, that either metaphysics or epistemology can relieve us of this condition. The problem is that these efforts are contingent too—they amount to mere descriptions (Nietzsche's interpretations), and any description may be made to look bad by simply giving another description, and yet another, and so on, ad nauseum. But none of this means that we should just give up and admit nihilistic defeat. Rorty the pragmatist wants us to adopt something akin to Nietzsche's creative response to the abyss of absurdity. In Rorty's terms the response is to accept the fact of radical contingency and then, in a spirit of irony, to go on inventing our own projects of self-creation. Our lives may then come to satisfy the psychological criterion for meaning. And if we keep up our conversations with other self-creators, there may arise some fortuitous measure of overlap between our subjective meanings. This is the best we can hope to achieve in our quest for a meaningful human existence.

The Illusion of Meaning

Introduction

At the heart of this chapter, and the next, is a debate about the reality of teleology, *so that* causality. Are telē real causal factors or not? Inherentists claim that goals and purposes are real, and they back up the claim by giving telē an important role in metaphysical systems. Telē, they believe, exist in the extra-mental world and they can be apprehended by objective inquiry or by revelation. Inventionists dismiss the claims of inherentism, insisting that telē are real only in the sense of existing in individual minds or in the collective meanings of groups, and they arise by creative imagination or by social intercourse. Are these purposes therefore not *really* real? Inventionists aren't much concerned about this question because it is motivated by metaphysical dogma, and inventionists don't go in much for metaphysics. Inventionists begin philosophical reflection with a presumption that subjective experience is real, and they don't bother to fortify the belief by playing metaphysical language games. Despite a fundamental difference in their metaphysical commitments, inherentists and inventionists agree that *so that* causality is essential for making a wide swath of important phenomena intelligible, and this is enough to distinguish them sharply from teleological reductionists.

Reductionism comes in different forms, but the basic idea is expressed in the language of "nothing but." If I say "X is nothing but Y," then I am claiming that there is nothing to X that isn't covered by Y, thus X is reducible to Y. The different forms of reductionism come to light when we ask what sorts of items Xs and Ys might be. *Methodological reductionism* is the weakest and least controversial form, amounting simply to a general principle of analysis. "Analysis" means "to dissolve," and the basic method in all domains of intellectual inquiry is to dissolve wholes into their constituent parts, enabling the parts to be studied independently. The goal of methodological reductionism is to render wholes more intelligible by coming to understand their parts. *Theoretical* (or epistemological) *reductionism* comes into play when the Xs and Ys are representations such as terms, concepts, categories, theories, or models. To illustrate, if someone were to claim that "chemistry (X) is nothing but physics (Y)," then the sense of the claim would be that the formulations of chemistry add nothing to what is already implicit in the formulations of physics, or that the theoretical corpus of chemistry performs no explanatory work that cannot be performed by the more fundamental theories of physics. Theoretical reductionism was captured in William of Ockham's "razor," giving us the principle that the simplest explanations—the ones involving fewest assumptions and abstractions—are always the best explanations. *Ontological reductionism* is focused on entities, events, properties, and relations that may or may not be real items. To perform an ontological reduction on some X is to show why beliefs about the X-entity (or X-property, etc.) should be eliminated in favor of beliefs about more fundamental entities, events, properties, and relations. For example, belief in the reality of a wet patch on the road ahead may be reduced to an illusion arising from the effects of heat and light on the visual system.

Teleological reductionists are prepared to weigh in on all three fronts. Methodologically, they will insist (uncontroversially) that breaking phenomena down to their constituent parts is fundamental to all serious inquiry and problem solving, and should be pursued by all available means. Epistemologically, they will argue that *so that* explanations involving goals, functions and purposes perform no explanatory work that isn't better and more precisely done by the *because of* dynamics of physics and chemistry. And when teleological explanations are grounded in metaphysical notions about essence or divine command or holistic properties, reductionists will try to give reasons why belief in these putative realities should be abandoned in favor of beliefs involving entities, events, properties, and relations having better ontological credentials.

The extreme reductionist position is that meaning is neither in the world nor in the mind, it is an illusion. The vocabulary of teleology may suit our desires for shorthand accounts of things, but in any true and complete description of reality the notion of *so that* causality would drop out of the picture without remainder.

Ancient Atomism

The atomistic theory developed in fifth century BCE Greece by Leucippus and Democritus is the earliest known attempt to articulate a comprehensive philosophical system without reference to teleological principles. According to ancient atomism, everything that happens happens *because of* undirected prior events. Leucippus is usually given credit for first expressing the atomist doctrine—reality is nothing but atoms and the void—while Democritus is remembered for elaborating the doctrine.[9]

Nothing but atoms and the void! The universe is eternal and without spatial limits. It is constituted by an infinite number of indivisible, indestructible, eternal, and imperceptibly small material atoms of various shapes. The atoms have been in motion from eternity within an infinite space, or void. Atoms bounce around in the void in ways that are determined by the force exerted on them by other atoms. There was no attempt by the atomists to formulate universal laws of motion—each movement of each atom owed its behavior entirely to whatever unique velocity and directionality of force was brought to it by contact with other atoms. Atoms occasionally congregate in clusters, forming composite objects that endure for a period of time. Until, that is, the clusters are busted up and dispersed by collisions with other meandering atoms. If a lot of smooth atoms get together they might accidentally form what an observer would identify as a body of water with the property of wetness, or if a bunch of jagged atoms got stuck tightly together the observer might identify a rock with the property of hardness. But the observer would be deluded in both cases because he/she would *not* perceive what is really there: nothing but tiny atoms with no qualitative properties at all, just the quantitative properties of shape and motion.

Democritus developed an elaborate account of physical objects, including humans capable of experience. Human bodies and minds are alike constructed from collections of material atoms. The mind is a physical organ, differing from other composite structures merely by virtue of the number, shapes, and motions of its constituent atoms. Here's a sketch of the way perception works. We start with an object of perception, say, a tree. The tree is nothing but atoms stuck together, enduring bombardments from other atoms that eventually knock loose poorly secured atoms. Now we have atoms moving in all directions from the vicinity of the tree, and some of these may, perchance, alight upon other clusters of atoms, like an eyeball, for example. Atoms impinging on the eyeball cause a chain reaction of motion in neighboring atoms until, perchance, the atoms composing the mind cluster are put into a particular pattern of motion experienced as "seeing a tree." It's all a giant illusion, of course, because the tree is really nothing but a coincidence of atoms in motion. And for its part, the mind is nothing but the same sort of derivative structure. Experiences thus occur, but there is no "experiencer," no independent self, just the rigidly determined behavior of discrete atoms. And there is no meaning involved. Atoms are not *about* anything at all. They have no telos, no inner agenda of values to account for their movements. They are completely passive in their reactions to the immediate past.

The astonishing thing is that Democritus worked these principles into a (sort of) moral theory. Experiences may be judged positive or negative, depending entirely, of course, on hits to the mind cluster from without. Different configurations of hits will determine whether the resulting experiences are good or bad. A mind cluster may also experience a preference for good over bad (again, depending on the hits received). Now, all of this action is completely objective, so that if a mind could "know" enough about the behavior of atoms it might be able to predict how things will go, experience-wise, and take measures to prepare the mind. At this point it appears that telē are sneaking into the picture ("take measures"? To what point?). But Democritus had this covered: whatever measures are taken happen *because of* undirected collisions from without. Again, it's all a grand illusion having no more meaning than specks of dust being buffeted by the breeze.

Hobbes

Early modern philosophers found themselves in an intellectual jam. On one hand, they wholeheartedly supported the expulsion of final causes from the domain of scientific inquiry, but on the other hand they could see that the domain of moral philosophy was moribund without telē. Science could not thrive *with* final causes, and the moral order could not survive *without* them. The most plausible solution to this problem appeared to be the Cartesian one: to divorce the realm of nature (matter, efficient causes) from the human realm (mind, final causes), but then to insist that reason ruled supreme in both realms.

But Thomas Hobbes wasn't buying it. Among modern philosophers Hobbes and Spinoza were the most critical of *so that* explanations and the most insistent on *because of* causal determinism. Hobbes was deeply impressed with the geometrical methods employed in scientific reasoning. The key to understanding how things work, he thought, was to form axioms by careful observation and then to reason deductively from these axioms. Hobbes believed that it was possible to reconstruct the entire scope of human knowledge along such geometrical lines. He was sympathetic with the atomistic doctrine that reality is nothing but material bodies in motion, but instead of describing the motion of imperceptibly small atoms, Hobbes fixed on three types of observable bodies: physical bodies, animal bodies, and political bodies. He also differed substantially from the atomists in his belief that there existed universal laws that governed the motion of bodies. The laws governing the motions of physical bodies were well described by Galileo, but it remained to give a geometrical account of the laws governing animal bodies and political bodies.[10]

Hobbes recognized two kinds of motion in animal bodies: *vital* (reflexes) and *voluntary* (cognition, deliberation). He described both types in strictly mechanical terms—whatever happens in vital and voluntary motions can in principle be traced to minute perturbations of matter within the organism. And all such perturbations were held to conform invariably to natural laws. Reasoning, for Hobbes, amounted to straightforward mechanical computation. But now we want to ask about the character of these psychological laws, for if telē were going to sneak into the dynamics of bodies in motion this would certainly be the place for them.

In the most fundamental terms, Hobbes argued, the motions of animal bodies can be described as movements either toward or away from other objects. Attractive motions are called *appetites*, while repulsive motions are *aversions*, and together these elementary motions describe what Hobbes calls "endeavors." Sensations, emotions, memories, cognition—these are all endeavors performed to preserve a body's state and to resist the powers of external causes to destroy it. "Performed to preserve?" Does a body endeavor *so that* it will persist? Is this teleology? One might think so, but again, Hobbes isn't buying it. Organisms behave *because of* prior causes only, and the phenomena of endeavoring are no exceptions. In Hobbes's thinking, the concept of endeavor is no different than the concept of inertia applied to the motion of physical bodies.

The concept of endeavoring provides the axiomatic basis for Hobbes's moral and political theory as well as for his psychology. Moral concepts of good and evil are thoroughly naturalized by equating them with appetites and aversions. The good is whatever attracts, and evil is whatever averts. The social contract theory developed at length by Hobbes amounts to a further elaboration of the endeavoring principle. Bodies are moved to preserve themselves, which drives them to escape the war-like dangers inherent in the state of nature and to seek peace, which compels them to commit to peacemaking contractual arrangements with other bodies. For Hobbes, then, the behavior of human beings is reducible to non-teleological dynamics, no less than the behavior of inanimate bodies has proven to be. We remain, of course, vulnerable to illusions about the reality of goals and purposes. When, for example, the consequence of some particular activity is a pleasurable feeling, we might erroneously conclude that pleasure was the *point* of the activity. In reality, however, such purposes do not exist, either in the world or in the mind.

Contemporary Reductionism

It's pretty clear that reductionism has carried the day with respect to causal dynamics at the level of inanimate objects. These days only a fool would declare that rivers cut through landscapes *so that* they might reach the sea, or that smoke rises *so that* it might escape through the hole at the apex of a teepee. It is also clear that reductionism has earned its bragging rights in the more recent debate over the putative involvement of intelligent agency in macroevolutionary events. Intelligent design advocates have challenged the standard Darwinian account of evolution with examples of biological mechanisms which, they say, are way too complex to be accounted for on Darwinian principles. The only way to make the appearance of such complexity intelligible, the argument goes, is to assume the intervention of an intelligent and purposeful causal agency. None of these challenges, however, has managed to stick. One by one, they have been decisively answered, with the ironic consequence that their efforts to weaken Darwinism have ultimately reinforced it. The debate is finished, and reductionism has won.

Several more interesting debates, however, continue unabated. These have to do with whether the phenomena of living systems themselves can be made intelligible apart from the causal logic of teleology. Can the biology and behavior of organisms, however simple or complex, be reduced to the dynamics of physics and chemistry? Is it possible, even in principle, to satisfy all nontrivial questions about biological adaptations and functions without recourse to *so that* dynamics? And perhaps the thorniest and most consequential debate of all: Can the intentionality of conscious experience make sense apart from the language of agency, value, and purpose? To all these questions reductionists give a resounding *Yes.*

Reductionism posits that all the causal arrows point upward throughout the hierarchy of material organization, and all the explanatory arrows point downward. Suppose you want a complete explanation of some complex phenomenon, say, a war. A reductionist analysis would go something like this. Wars consist of social groups deploying machines against one another with the intention of achieving a specific telos: victory. The full explanation of war machines (inanimate objects) is covered by routine classical mechanics. As for societies, they are composed of individual parts (persons), which are in turn composed of organs and tissues, which are reducible to cells constituted by macromolecules. Once we arrive at the level of macromolecules we are well into the realm of inanimate objects, where all the explanatory principles belong properly to the disciplines of physics and chemistry, from which disciplines all rumors of warful goals and purposes vanish without trace. Telē, on this view, amount to nothing but shorthand conventions that refer, ultimately, to the dynamics of particles in motion.

Reductionism appears to have time on its side. By this I mean that the peculiar logic of final causality gives the appearance of backward causation. Telē may be specified in terms of future states (which don't yet exist), so the claim that telē are real causes seems to imply that a nonexistent future state may cause a present event, and such claims are counterintuitive, to say the least. Of course, defenders of teleological causality will insist that it does not entail backward causation, but the impression that it does is enough to leave teleologists with some serious explaining to do. Reductionists, however, don't find the explanations very convincing.

One of the strongest and most explicit versions of contemporary reductionism is known as "eliminative materialism," a position associated with the neuroscience duo, Paul and Patricia Churchland. The arguments of eliminativists have zeroed in on the inadequacy of folk psychology, our intuitive notions about the dynamics of human behavior. Commonsense folk psychology makes use of concepts such as beliefs, desires, goals, values, and intentions, and it also makes tacit assumptions concerning law-like relations among these phenomena— all in the service of making predictions about human behavior. Paul Churchland argues that folk psychology therefore qualifies as a theory. But it's not a good one. In fact, folk psychology is such a bad theory that it deserves outright elimination, rather than piecemeal translation to a more basic theory:

What we must say is that [folk psychology] suffers explanatory failures on an epic scale, that it has been stagnant for at least twenty-five centuries, and that its categories appear (so far) to be incommensurable with or orthogonal to the categories of the background physical science whose long-term claim to explain human behavior seems undeniable. Any theory that meets this description must be allowed a serious candidate for outright elimination.[11]

It's not that beliefs, desires and telē are nothing but something else, it's rather that they are nothing but sorry illusions. And for the same reasons that science has eliminated failed theories about phlogiston, the ether, vital forces, and the four humors, it should also eliminate teleological concepts. In place of the discarded vocabulary and ontology of folk psychology there will arise the true language of a completed neuroscience, enabling us to say what is *really* on our minds, that is, nothing but neurons and neurotransmitters.

3

The Emergence of Meaning

The purpose of this chapter is to set out an emergence perspective on meaning as a serious alternative to the perspectives examined in the previous chapter. It will be my aim to do this in a way that combines the strengths of inherentism, inventionism, and reductionism while avoiding their problematic aspects. If this were a multiple-choice question the options would be these:

A. Meaning is in the world (inherentism)

B. Meaning is in the mind (inventionism)

C. Meaning is neither in the world nor in the mind (reductionism)

D. All of the above, more or less (emergentism)

The correct answer, in my view, is D. At first sight this may appear to be an impossible option, as the first three options have the appearance of being incommensurable. But if we consider that each of these options varies in a range from strong to weak versions, then we might come to view them as overlapping perspectives. And this should allow us to work aspects of each into a coherent compromise perspective on the meaning of life.

What Is Emergence?

All emergentist thinkers sign on to the following two principles:

1. The material world consists of levels of organization, such that lower-level systems (prior, normally less complex)

are necessary conditions for the existence of emergent, higher-level systems.

2. Higher-level systems manifest emergent properties (structures, patterns, behaviors) that are not predictable from, or reducible to, our knowledge of the properties and dynamics of lower-level systems.

Strong emergentists will add a third, ontological, principle:

3. Higher-level systems constitute novel *realities* (not merely appearances), having novel causal influence, and calling for the formulation of new laws of nature.

I will be supporting a strong version of emergentism, and since the strong form has more controversial implications it will be useful to explore these principles a bit further. We might begin by getting the *grunge* out, by which I mean the "grunge theory" of matter. There is nothing at all scientific about the grunge theory of matter—it's basically a vague metaphysical notion, an example of folk philosophy that has achieved the status of common sense. The grunge theory has a low estimation of matter: matter isn't much, it's just grunge, just crude uninteresting stuff. Matter *becomes* interesting only when the laws of nature whip it into shape. The grunge theory gives us the dualistic view that matter and the laws of nature are somehow independent—grunge in one dimension, eternal laws in another—and we cannot expect an orderly creation until the laws of nature come to bear upon the grunge. This is the picture we find enshrined in the biblical story of creation: in the beginning there was nothing but misty chaos (grunge) until God laid down the law. The same view is found in Plato's *Timaeus*, where the demiurge is given the role of ordering the physical world by bringing it, as nearly as possible, into conformity with transcendent reason.

But there is another view—I'll call it the "glitz theory" of matter—that is more compatible with emergence thinking. The glitz theory basically says that there are *no eternal laws of nature*. That is, laws of nature do not exist independently of matter. Matter alone is sufficient. On this view, all we have in the real world is *matter* and its *properties*. What looks to us like a law of nature is really nothing more than our attempt to describe regularities in the properties of matter. The properties of matter are not endowed from the outside.

We see something like the glitz theory in Aristotle's cosmology. He unified matter and form in the concept of substance: *formed matter*. Nowhere do we find matter without properties of form, and (contra Plato) nowhere do we find form without matter.

If one accepts the glitz theory of matter, then it is easier to see the possibility that genuinely new properties of matter might arise spontaneously—properties that could never be predicted from the properties we previously knew about. A classic example is the buoyancy of ice. Buoyancy is not a property of water in its liquid or gaseous states, but when you freeze water you alter relationships between the molecules, giving rise to a novel phenomenon. Buoyancy is a *real* property, but it's an emergent one, a *system* property, not simply more of what was there before. That is, an omniscient description of the properties of hydrogen and oxygen would not include a description of buoyancy.

Strong emergence theory embodies a thesis about *reality*. Whereas ontological reductionism claims that high-level complex systems are merely piled-up simplicities ("more of the same"), emergentism invites us to see that nature is often more *than* the same. Genuine novelty, it says, may be real-ized (made real) as relationships among the constituent parts of a system change. The emergence story is about transcendence, but not of the "skyhook" variety. This story invites us to see that nothing transcends nature like nature itself.

The emergence thesis is really quite simple on the surface, but terribly complex in the details. It basically says that it is possible for matter to create the circumstances in which new material properties arise spontaneously. And when new properties arise, of course, new laws of nature come into play. New lawful properties allow even more complex structures and relations to occur, increasing the probability that additional—completely unforeseeable—novelty might arise, again changing probabilities for further properties to emerge, and so on, and on. The hierarchical structure we observe in the natural world—subatomic particles, atoms, molecules, cells, tissues, organs, organisms, populations, communities—is precisely the sort of cosmology one would expect to find if the emergence thesis were true.

Now we come to the most controversial, and strangely paradoxical, implication of the strong emergence thesis. The claim is that the dynamics of teleological causality are emergent. That is, the *so that* logic underlying goals, purpose, agency, intentionality, function, and meaning amounts to a novel mode of causality in the universe. Prior to the emergence of this new causal dynamic in living systems, everything that happened in the universe followed the *because of* logic of efficient causality. No telē, no meanings. For billions of years the universe was completely void of meaningful events. But then, quite unpredictably, the odds favoring a new kind of causality came within reach. The astonishing claim here is that a pointless process created the conditions for the pointfulness of biological functions. A universe with no telos, a universe without an agenda, just *inadvertently* made possible the spontaneous emergence of purposeful activity. Accidental intentionality? Imagine that!

In fact, there are many who cannot imagine it. It seems a lot easier to write teleology off as an illusion, as strong reductionists do. And if one is instead going to be a realist about telē, then why not build them into the fabric of the cosmos from the get-go, as inherentists do? Whitehead's inherentism led him to reject early versions of emergence proposed by the British philosophers Samuel Alexander and C. D. Broad. And theologian John Haught dismisses the emergence of teleology as mere superstition and magic.[1] If we take seriously David Hume's admonition that extraordinary claims require extraordinary evidence, then it would appear that strong emergentists have their work cut out for them. The problem is to show how the conditions for the emergence of teleology might have come about. It's not enough to wave a hand while keeping a straight face. Later in this chapter we will have an opportunity to examine Terrence Deacon's efforts to bring rigor to the emergence thesis.

For the moment we might briefly note that extraordinary claims are fairly ordinary fare in the history of science. Think about what Copernicus was up against. And Darwin. And what about the proposal that the universe originated in a Big Bang? Or consider the extraordinary nature of the claim that the four fundamental forces of nature were at one point unified. If a plurality of fundamental forces can arise from a primordial unity, then there should be no a priori reason to reject claims about emergent laws and causal properties in nature. Stranger things have been proposed.

Revisiting the Options

I have promised to advance our inquiry into the meaning of life in a manner that brings together elements of inherentism, inventionism, and reductionism. Each of these perspectives offers useful insights for our inquiry, but each has serious limitations as well. The strategy followed here will be to gather up what is useful and leave the rest behind.

Reductionism

One of the most lamentable aspects of contemporary culture is the casual and uncritical use of dismissive labels. Ever since the Reagan era the word *liberal* has offered an effective means for demonizing political opponents, whether they are liberal or not. The "reductionist" label carries with it the same opprobrium. In popular discourse reductionism is a downer, and reductionists themselves tend to be viewed as ogres and spoilers. The unfortunate irony of this bias is that few things have been more beneficial to human welfare than the spirit of reductionism. All serious inquiry, all problem solving, is rigorously reductionist. Wherever we can point to the liberation of humankind from the darkness of ignorance and superstition we have reductionism to thank. The very first step in constructive thinking is reductive analysis. Our bias, therefore, should always be in favor of reductionism, and we ought enthusiastically to encourage inquirers to be as thorough in their reductions as possible. This bias should apply to all forms of reductionism: methodological, epistemological, and ontological. The question about reductionism, therefore, is not whether its goals ought to be pursued—they obviously should—but whether specific claims to reduction can be justified.

The most extreme form of ontological reductionism would claim that our ontological categories should exclude all but the most fundamental entities, events, properties, and relations. If we take this extreme position, then we find ourselves committed to the doctrine that the only real entities are quarks (or strings), the only real properties are those of quarks (or strings), the only real relations are those among quarks (or strings), and the only real events are quark (or string) events. This view implies, of course, that water molecules are not "really" real because they are nothing but atoms of hydrogen and oxygen, and these elements are not "real" either, because they are nothing but quarks (or strings). No one in their right mind holds this silly view. The more common (and plausible) form of extreme reductionism claims that since quarks (or strings) are the most fundamental realities we know, it follows that if anything is real it is composed, ultimately, of quarks (or strings). That is, all realities are *at least* quark (or string) derivatives. This version makes a lot of sense, and it amounts to an expression of metaphysical materialism, the view that if something is material it is real, and if something is real it is material. This form of ontological reductionism (i.e., materialism) will accept the reality of hydrogen atoms, water molecules, mountain streams, wedding receptions, economic recoveries, and so on.

The specific reductionistic claim that interests our inquiry is whether attributions of goal-seeking behavior can be successfully reduced to non-teleological terms, whether meaning can be reduced to absurdity. In keeping with the spirit of reductionism, we should be eager to dismiss teleological attributions wherever we are justified in doing so. For example, we have good reason to dismiss claims that rivers, storm systems, forest fires, earthquakes, and the like, are intentional phenomena. To attribute agency to these phenomena is to commit the fallacy of anthropomorphism. The same thing goes for claims of agency *behind* these phenomena. Thus, the assertion that hurricane Katrina was God's retribution for the sins of New Orleans goes down as ridiculous (as well as vicious). The spirit of reductionism calls us to proceed always with a presumption of non-telos. The burden of proof justifiably falls on those who advance teleological attributions.

Steven Weinberg was proceeding with a presumption of non-telos when he famously remarked that the more we learn about the cosmos the less reason we have to believe that it serves a purpose.[2] Weinberg wasn't thinking about human beings when he said this; he was, rather, thinking about the universe as a whole. Basically, he was dismissing the inherentist claim that there is a telos woven into the fabric of the cosmos. And, frankly, the more we learn about the cosmos the more reason we have to believe that Weinberg was right. The universe, taken as a whole, is a long process of constructive and destructive material change, but none of it bears the marks of goal-directedness. It might be compared to a huge bus that is going . . . nowhere. It just goes, destinationless, according to the telos-free laws of physics and chemistry. If we had to assign a purpose to the universe it would have to be the goal of maximizing entropy. But such a "purpose" is completely explainable in terms of physics and chemistry, and is therefore reducible.

Weinberg's reduction of cosmic purpose—his cosmic nihilism—is a perfectly reasonable position to take, and one that we would do well to endorse in the course of our inquiry. The universe as a whole is a meaningless affair, the bus is going nowhere. But cosmic nihilism does not entail that all attributions of purpose are necessarily unjustified. The bus may be going nowhere, but this doesn't mean that occupants of the bus cannot go to and fro filled with genuine goals. The fact—if it is one—that the universe is a meaningless affair does not reduce my life to a meaningless affair. It simply means that my purposes have no cosmic significance. But why should that deflate my quest for a meaningful life? Do human ends have to serve cosmic ends in order to be genuine? A lot of inherentists appear to think so. Thus, we often hear people make the extraordinary claim that if God does not exist then there is no point to human existence. Such claims may make sense on the assumption that God endowed humans with a purpose, but in the absence of compelling evidence for this we should accept it as a given that the spirit of reductionism has stripped the cosmos of inherent telē, and in doing so it has stripped our telē of cosmic significance. And for this we should be grateful to reductionism, for it relieves us of the awesome burden of taking ourselves too seriously. But we should not take the Weinbergian thesis to count as a dismissal of genuine teleological phenomena *within* the universe. And this refusal puts us in the company of a majority of biologists.

Before getting caught up in the biology we need to be clear about what attributions of teleological behavior do and do not claim. When I say that John acts *so that* he might achieve a goal I am not suggesting that his behavior somehow circumvents or neutralizes *because of* dynamics. Far from it. We may accept fully the view that human beings are material entities, which means that John is *at least* quarks (or strings), which further means that there must always be a *because of* story going on. There should be no dispute about any of that. The controversial question is whether the *because of* story is sufficient, that is, whether it succeeds in rendering John's behavior fully intelligible. The strong emergence thesis wants to say that there is also a *so that* story going on—one that makes the details of the *because of* story as rich as they are. If there is such a story, then it cannot proceed in a way that contradicts any details of the *because of* account. *So that* dynamics (if they're really in play) must go forward within the constraints of *because of* dynamics. It's a question of whether there are *relational* details involved in the behavior that exceed the explanatory resources of physics and chemistry. That is, are there emergent system properties at work that cannot be captured in descriptions of lower-level systems (recall the buoyancy effect)? The strong emergence thesis says Yes, and it offers biological functionality as a challenge to the strong reductionist thesis. If the strong reductionist thesis is true, then physics and chemistry should be able to give a complete account of biological functions (including human agency) without using teleological language—but this is what emergentism says it cannot do. And if strong reductionism fails, then purposeful agency deserves to be recognized as a real phenomenon in nature, not merely an illusion.

The literature on this topic in the philosophy of biology is vast and complicated, to say the least. But it all seems to boil down to whether or not the physical sciences can provide a completely satisfying account of the phenomena of *adaptation*. There is no problem in the case of rivers adjusting to their landscapes as they run to the sea. The physical sciences don't even blink on that problem. But the adaptation of organisms to their environments is not so simple. The course a river takes may be described as an *accidental effect*, following geological constraints on water flow, but for organisms adaptation is a matter of *functional effects*. Here's the difference: making the "lub-dub" sound is an accidental effect of the heart, but pumping blood is a functional effect. Biologists can't get along without the concept of function—it informs analysis and explanation at every level, from individual cells to ecosystems. And the working definition of function in biology is explicitly teleological: a function is what a trait (a structure or behavior) is *supposed to do*. The function of a heart, for example, is to pump blood, it is *for* or *about* pumping blood.

This working definition of function is worrisome to many philosophers both because it appears to entail backward causation and because it appears to presume an element of design. To address these worries, philosophers of biology took to explaining function by recourse to natural selection: functional traits came to be, not because they were meant to be *for* something, but merely because those organisms that accidentally had them were better able to survive and reproduce. The Darwinian account of evolution by natural selection is able to explain how new traits arise without the presumption of foresight or design. But the teleological language remains: functional traits are there because in the past they served the *goal* of reproductive fitness. Natural selection provides powerful tools for explaining specific modifications in living systems, but it doesn't offer a complete explanation for the origins of life. Evolutionary theory *assumes* the teleological nature of living systems.

Our question now goes straight to the origins of life. Any way you cut it, biological traits do whatever they do *so that* organisms might resist becoming playthings of the environment (like rivers, or *der Muselmann*). So the question is whether or not life itself is an emergent process that transcends the explanatory powers of the physical sciences. This question will not be settled any time soon. At the end of the day a plausible strong reductionist account of the origin of life might come forward, but presently the prospects are not encouraging. Meanwhile, we already have several promising emergentist models for the origin of life (see the Deacon model ahead). For the moment, at least—insofar as living organisms are concerned—the presumption of non-telos must give way to a presumption of emergent teleology.

Where does this leave us? We might say that a responsible emergence theory of meaning is comfortable with the reductionist rejection of purpose at the level of the universe taken as a whole, but that there is good reason to accept the objective reality of purposeful agency operating within the dynamics of living systems. The bus may not be going anywhere, but we are.

Inherentism

The inherentist doctrine says that meaning exists objectively in the world—that it is there to be discovered, or perhaps revealed. It now appears that our reductionist bias has ruled out inherentism at the cosmic level, but has left a remnant of it intact at the level of living organisms. It may not be inherentism full-blown, perhaps, but it's something. Now, we might ask to what extent we can allow ourselves to be enthusiastic inherentists. We are left with the idea that life itself is an emergent teleological process. Meaning is in the world, then, in the measure to which living organisms are governed by inherent purposes. If we are interested in discovering the meaning of life we will have to determine what those inherent purposes are.

It seems best to begin at the most general level of all: What are living organisms for? We are given the happy circumstance that there exists a virtual consensus about this among biologists: living organisms are for achieving reproductive fitness. That's ultimately what all those complicated adaptations are about: survival and reproduction. All species have special interests, they are programmed to prefer certain conditions, they seek out and thrive under these conditions—these are all ways to speak about the evaluative functions emerging in living systems as a result of natural selection. In short, agency and motivation can be claimed as universal characteristics of life. Living things are motivated to seek out or to create the conditions that are favorable to their carrying on. Life is motivated matter.

Wherever life exists the conditions for viability are valued. The claim that viability is a universal telos embodied in all living things comes close to being a necessary truth. One might be tempted to say that the value of viability is universal, objective, and ultimate. In fact, I confess to a high level of comfort with all three of these claims. Yet none of them finds favor among the holders of informed opinion these days, so a defense may be in order. Before defending these claims about the value of viability, however, I should clarify what I mean by the term. I take viability to mean something very close to the literal sense, that is, "likely or able to live." To value viability is to value the continuation and fulfillment of life. For our purposes the value of viability may be seen to include the values expressed in the struggle of individuals of all species to survive as well as the values expressed in efforts of all species to achieve reproductive success.

Now to defend the claims that viability is a universal, objective, and ultimate value. The claim for universality says that organisms of all species have it in their nature to optimize viability. The claim for objectivity says that all behaviors to the contrary may be judged with confidence to be wrong in the sense of being maladaptive. And the claim for ultimacy says that viability is a necessary condition for all other values.

Those intent on denying the claim for universality will draw attention to alleged exceptions among humans. Here may be found examples taken from religious traditions claiming that the true meaning of life is not in the living but rather in the transcendence of life. Christians, for example, are often encouraged to care less for the prospect of life than for the prospects after death. The life one has in the natural order has value merely as a means to a more ultimate form of supernatural existence. In itself, viability is hollow and without enduring promise. In this example—and there are many others like it—we appear to be given decisive reason to drop the claim that viability is universally valued.

But things are not always as they appear. It is important not to confuse verbal expressions of the meaning of life with the tacit, embodied value of viability. When individuals articulate the meaning of life they are attempting to specify *why they value life*. Those inspired with Christian hope may insist that life has no meaning or value apart from the prospect of transcending it. On the surface this may be seen as a rejection of the ultimate value of viability, but in fact it may be only one of many particular ways to affirm viability. For example, it is common for individuals to claim that life has no meaning apart from their families, friends, work, hobbies, and so on. And it is true that the loss of one's job or a loved one (or the loss of religious faith) may pitch a life into despair, but in the course of time persons normally find a way to reconstruct meaning in their lives. Even when the particular sources of life's meaning are lost, we are able to find the will to reconstruct meaning. It is this deep reserve of motivation that I mean by the universal value of viability. There may indeed be a rich plurality of particular reasons given for valuing life, but this is no evidence against a universally embodied value that functions as the ultimate source of these diverse meanings.

One further note about religion: whatever religious memes appear to say on the surface, it is reasonable to view them as devices designed for optimizing the continuation of life. That is, these meanings normally function as instruments for generating and reinforcing the kinds of attitudes and behaviors that are adaptive in the evolutionary sense. This is precisely what we should expect once we admit that culture itself is a complex biological adaptation—that is, a collection of shared meanings that assist our species in meeting the challenges to viability. Religious systems have emerged as cultural artifacts because they have proven to be biologically significant. Thus, despite appearances to the contrary, religious memes exist in service to the ultimate value of viability.

Next comes the defense of moral objectivity and ultimacy. I have said that any behaviors contrary to the value of viability may be judged to be objectively wrong. That is to say, the standard of viability is ultimately what *makes* something right or wrong. Bold and unambiguous claims of this sort have the appearance of simplifying the moral life, but nothing could be farther from the truth. Having a crisp and objective moral standard does not mean that particular moral judgments will themselves be objective, or even easy. Even if we agree that viability is an objective value there will remain plenty of room for disagreement about which behaviors might or might not advance it. The moral life is always messy.

But can it be agreed that viability is an objective value? Anyone making a claim for the objectivity of any value must sooner or later come to terms with the infamous *naturalistic fallacy*. In the eighteenth century, David Hume warned us of the dangers of this fallacy. It is fallacious, he insisted, to derive value claims from objective factual claims. Facts (i.e., accounts of how things are) constitute one sort of thing, but values (i.e., appraisals of which things matter) constitute quite another sort—and the two are incommensurable. No matter how deeply one is committed to a moral value, there is no way to establish the value by a demonstration of facts alone. There must be at least one given, or assumed, value. To illustrate: we cannot infer *from* "consuming cyanide causes death" *to* "one should not consume cyanide." To be valid the inference requires an intervening value assumption, such as, "death is bad." Once the intervening assumption is allowed, the inference can go forward. But facts alone cannot establish the objectivity of values, any more than wishing for something makes it come true. Ever since Hume the prevailing view among moral philosophers has been that there are no demonstrably objective values. This suggests that one may take a moral stand against the value of viability without fear of inconsistency.

At this point I need to make one thing clear. In most cases (all but one, actually), I agree with those who cite the naturalistic fallacy in opposing invalid claims for the objectivity of moral values. But there is something so extraordinary about the fact that all species are geared up for the purpose of living that I find it reasonable to make an exception. In other words, I believe we are justified—the naturalistic fallacy notwithstanding—in asserting viability as the one and only objective moral standard.

Here are my reasons. It seems clear that moral reasoning depends on what might be called moral imagination, that is, the ability to generate a variety of options for behavior together with the ability to winnow them selectively on the basis of moral sensibilities. Apart from these abilities nothing about moral discourse makes any sense. This said, we may now ask about *the value of these abilities themselves*. If moral imagination is a good thing—as all moralists must believe— then what *makes* it a good thing? The biologically informed answer would be that moral imagination serves an adaptive purpose, that is, it is instrumentally valuable in helping our species to meet the challenges to viability. This means that the value of moral reasoning per se derives from the value of viability. But if the value of having a range of behavioral options is relative to viability, then the value assigned to any particular option is also determined relative to the standard of viability, and if the value of every moral option (together with the ability to imagine a range of options) is relative to the same standard, then that standard may be said to be objective. If one therefore chooses to act in ways that contradict the value of viability, one thereby chooses contrary to the conditions of one's choosing. I believe this qualifies as an objectively irrational act.

There is little to be gained by wandering farther into abstract philosophical disputes. The important point is that the value of viability deserves special status in the attempt to discover what living organisms (including humans) are for. It is the one value that commands all others. Indeed, I have given sufficient reasons for thinking it is irrational to affirm any value as more binding or less optional than this one. If anything matters, then what matters most is viability. To sum up: it is wrong always, everywhere, and for anyone, to value anything above the enduring prospect of life.

We now have before us the ultimate purpose of life: the continuation and fulfillment of life. Dare we to ask about the value of recognizing such an idea? For all this lofty talk about the inherent value of viability, what difference does it make in the actual business of living? Even if it is granted that viability is an objective and ultimate value for all life forms, the fact remains that it is hardly ever recognized as such. Certainly not by mussels and magpies. And even among humans a recognition of viability as the ultimate value is rare. The reason is that viability is an abstraction, far too generalized to be of much use in the struggle for survival. Who gets up in the morning with the intention of maximizing reproductive fitness? That is not the way it works. Instead, we wake up with more interesting and immediate goals in mind. We wake up from our night dreams only to take up our day dreams of love and hope and treasure seeking— these are the concerns that drive us from day to day. Winning the war may be the supreme goal, but as every general knows, all the action takes place at the level of particular battles. So it turns out that the ultimate value is often or even normally obscured by more proximate interests. And wisely so. Generals who try to win wars generally lose them. Nevertheless, it makes occasional good sense to focus on the ultimate goal as a way of restoring our perspective on immediate concerns. Sometimes it is important to crawl out of the trenches and consult the big picture. And who knows?—doing so might result in choosing different battles.

It may be true enough to say that the ultimate point of life is living, but certainly this goal is much too general to satisfy our inquiry. Asking the question at the most general level of all fails to distinguish the meaning of human life from all other forms of life. Ask a general question, get a general answer. Besides, the ultimate goal of viability doesn't take us very far in satisfying our original criteria for a meaningful life. I may, for example, be virtuous in serving the ultimate goal of viability, but this is hardly enough to make me happy.

How, then, would things look if we tried the question at the other extreme, at the level of concrete experienced meaning? We might engage a team of social scientists to go around asking individual human beings to tell us what constitutes meaning in their lives. Would this manner of putting the question help us to discover inherent meanings in the world? Not likely. At the individual level of experienced meaning there are too many answers, and it would be foolish to expect any of them to speak for all of humankind. The meaning of life at the individual level is far too variable for our interests.

What we're really asking is whether there are any telē that are inherent in *all* humans and *only* humans, and this brings us to a very controversial issue: *Is there a human nature?* So far we have committed ourselves—well, I have anyway—to a minimal inherentism: the essential point of all life is living. But if we can be convinced that there is an objective human nature, then our commitment to inherentism will be considerably expanded (not, however, all the way out to the cosmos). Here we need to be very careful, because any mention of "human nature" may call to mind the old-fashioned essentialism that gets postmodernists so worked up. We might be able to avoid the major difficulties by disavowing, up front, the idea that there are any eternally fixed characteristics that define what all human beings are for. The essentialist understanding of human nature was discredited once and for all by Darwin's demonstration that species are not fixed. This does not mean, however, that the species concept itself was rendered useless. It merely changed from absolute to statistical, from necessary to contingent, and from eternal to temporal. With this disclaimer firmly in place we may proceed, cautiously, to explore our human nature.

More Inherentism

If you want to apprehend the nature of a species you have to identify all of its functions, that is, the adaptive traits that are specified by the genome of the species. We may avoid the essentialism of yore by throwing in qualifiers such as, "for the relevant past, for here and now, and for the foreseeable future," and "for the vast statistical majority." Species are fluid, but the concept is pragmatically indispensable for inquiry. So if we want to apprehend the nature of human beings we need to attend to the adaptive traits encoded into the human genome. But it is extremely difficult to match up specific genetic profiles with specific structural and behavioral traits. In many cases we can already be precise. For example, we now have a specific genetic profile for the number of limbs, and another profile for eye color and others for blood types. But when you consider the complex nature of human anatomy and physiology, and when you add in the astonishing complexity and variation in human behavior, you tend to get humble pretty quickly about the prospect of constructing a precise genetic catalog of universal and unique human telē. What this tells us is that any comprehensive conclusions we come up with about human nature are going to be rather vague as well as temporary and statistical. Still, we know more than enough to silence the extreme deniers of human nature.

One way to get a handle on adaptive traits is to view them as anatomical, physiological, and behavioral strategies for achieving viability. For example, human anatomy conforms to a five-point body plan (head plus four limbs), an important element in our global strategy for carrying on. This is a universally human strategy, but it certainly isn't uniquely human, as any turtle will be quick to remind you. We share lots (and I mean *lots*) of such traits with other species. But as we get farther away in evolutionary time from our ancient common ancestors, we encounter our own distinctive strategies for carrying on.

To make an extremely long (and breathtakingly beautiful) story short, I will propose two telē that represent the universal uniqueness of human nature: *personal wholeness* and *social coherence*. The point is this: there are countless ways to pursue the holy grail of viability—that is, there are countless species—but the distinctively *human* way is simultaneously to achieve the goals of personality and sociality. Let me be clear: these are abstractions, like viability. There are no specific genetic profiles corresponding to the construction of personality and sociality. What I'm getting at here is that there *are* genetic sequences that code for the development of specific anatomical, physiological and behavioral traits, which collectively point to the global telē of personal wholeness and social coherence. I'm taking a rather large leap here in saying that all the particular functions we find among members of our species—including anatomical and physiological traits as well as behavior mediation systems, such as reflex systems, perceptual systems, drive systems, learning and memory systems, emotional systems, and cognitive systems—all these make contributions to achieving the *penultimate telē* of personal wholeness and social coherence, which in turn make decisive contributions to achieving the *ultimate telos* of reproductive fitness. If this is right, then there is reason to believe that we have discovered a second layer of meaning in the world. That is, inherent in our nature are the twin imperatives to construct healthy, autonomous individual personalities while simultaneously constructing cohesive, cooperative social groups. We are by nature a social species, composed of individuals having complex psychological needs.

What I mean most generally by personal wholeness is just the sorts of positive outcomes that are aimed for by *therapy* (broadly construed). And by social coherence I mean the sorts of positive outcomes that are aimed for by *politics* (broadly construed). Personal wholeness and social coherence are mutually depending and mutually contending goals. On one hand, they are interdependent values in the sense that each is a necessary condition for the other. Whole persons cannot be nurtured in a context of social chaos, and a cohesive social order cannot be constructed by dysfunctional individuals. It is clear that psychological problems can be addressed by social change, just as social problems can be addressed by psychological change. On the other hand, personal wholeness and social coherence are contenders in the sense that they have the potential to undermine one another. For example, individuals tend to lay excessive demands on social resources, while groups tend to make excessive demands for personal sacrifice.

The challenge of personal wholeness is to maximize the goods (goals) aimed at by our motivational systems and subsystems, while minimizing conflict between these systems. Whole persons are well nourished and free of debilitating diseases, they are fully engaged with the world, and have robust yet effectively managed motivational systems. These are persons who are able to construct agendas of sequential tasks, to anticipate outcomes, to assign priorities, and then attend to the most important matters while momentarily suppressing the demands of competing impulses. In short, whole persons are able to manage the demands placed on them by a plurality of potentially conflicting motivational systems. By harmonizing these demands they maximize their achievement of the goods aimed at by these systems.

The challenge of social coherence is not unlike the challenge of multicellularity—that is, how to get a plurality of discrete units to behave with a unity of purpose. The secret is to foster conditions for overlaps of self-interest and to minimize the potential for conflicts of self-interest. These elements constitute what Robert Wright has called "non-zero-sum" conditions.[3] A zero-sum game has clear winners and losers, but in a non-zero-sum game it is possible for everyone to come away a winner. It is impossible, given self-interest, to maintain non-zero-sum conditions perpetually, but our universal emotional toolkit helps us to regulate social interactions in ways that create just enough non-zero-sumness to keep social systems acceptably near equilibrium. It helps, surely, to be blessed with abundant resources and freedom from external threats, conditions that normally rely on a blend of luck and industry.

By means of various built-in mechanisms for behavior individuals have a decent chance of achieving a state of functional integrity against the odds inherent in a plurality of motivational systems (given a stable social order). And by means of built-in mechanisms for regulating social relationships societies have a decent chance of achieving a state of solidarity and cooperation against the odds inherent in a sea of self-interest (given the integrity of enough individuals).

The present state of the argument is that humans, like all other species, are equipped with traits designed by natural selection to pursue the ultimate telos of viability, and that the distinctively human strategy for doing this is to maintain a dynamic reciprocity between the dual goals of personal integrity and social solidarity. By harmonizing these objectives we optimize the prospects for human reproductive fitness.

All of this looks pretty reasonable as long as we move quickly and keep our eyes shut. But a moment's reflection will show us that there is something wrong here. The problem seems to be that these twin telē for achieving viability are not sufficiently unique to human beings. Dogs and buffalo and barnyard animals are all, like us, social species composed of individuals having complex psychological needs. All mammals, as well as several bird species, are equipped with emotional systems that function to regulate social dynamics. And for certain, the extent to which we share traits with the great apes is enough to undermine the claim that humans are unique in being geared up to seek personal wholeness and social coherence. Chimps and bonobos are built this way, too. If we wish to discover something special about human nature we will have to ask whether there is something sharply distinctive about the way humans pursue the twin telē.

The Emergence of Human Nature

The obvious answer is probably the best one: whereas nonhuman apes pursue the challenges of personality and sociality primarily by means of genetically ordained mechanisms for behavior, human apes pursue them by the extragenetic means of symbolic culture. The distinctiveness of human nature, therefore, must be tied in some way to our unique and innate capacity to create progressive cultural traditions. Again, this is probably the correct answer, but the important insights about human nature are buried in the details. The story is incompletely understood, but enough is known to warrant tentative hypotheses. I will here advance the proposal that cultural traditions, together with the most distinctive aspects of human nature, represent complex emergent phenomena.

Something dramatic happened between forty and fifty thousand years ago—a momentous event that archaeologists refer to as "the great leap forward." The archaeological remains of early humans prior to this period show very little evidence of diversity or innovation. The earliest tool sets and other artifacts look pretty much the same regardless of their location. Then quite suddenly the picture changes, revealing much more sophisticated and variable artifacts. This dramatic shift in material remains might very well signal the origin of progressive cultural traditions as well as a transformation in human nature. That there *was* a radical transformation in human nature at some point in the deep past is almost too obvious to deserve mention. When you compare the anatomy and physiology of chimps and humans you come away impressed with the stark similarities. Geneticists inform us that the genomes of humans and chimps vary by less than 3 percent, yet the differences in behavior are immense. Chimps are much more closely related to humans than to gorillas, but they surely don't act like it. So how did it happen that humans came to be the odd ape out? You might think that the great leap forward could be explained by the acquisition of language. Certainly, language was essential for the origins of cultural traditions, but the fact that humans were in full possession of language for 150,000 years before the great leap points to a different explanation.[4] Given the state of archaeological evidence, any "explanation" will be, of necessity, highly speculative, but here follows a fairly plausible one.

For the vast majority—over 99 percent—of human history our ancestors lived as hunter-gatherers, drifting around in small groups of two or three dozen closely related individuals. Normally, individuals would spend much of their time dispersed over a fairly large territory, periodically returning to a base camp. The occupancy of base camps might vary from a few days to a month, or perhaps longer if resources were abundant. As food supplies thinned out the group would move to a new base camp. This pattern of social organization is very similar to the one known by our chimpanzee cousins. Early human societies were maintained at low population density, seldom exceeding four or five individuals per square mile. Whenever the size of these wandering groups swelled beyond a few dozen individuals they would destabilize and subdivide into smaller groups.

The key to understanding the social organization of these groups is that the social glue holding them together was genetic. That is, interactions between individuals were governed by the logic of kin selection and the genetically scripted functioning of the so-called social emotions (including affection, gratitude, sympathy, anger, fear, and resentment). The gut reactions produced by these innate emotional systems constituted an implicit moral code. And this built-in morality was enough—as it is among chimps today—to assure group solidarity and cooperation by fostering overlaps of self-interest. Small-scale hunting-gathering groups lived, literally, from hand to mouth, a life based on instant gratification. They invested little and used the simplest of technologies. Everything was scaled to the campsite: they practiced a campsite economy, supported by a campsite technology and regulated by a campsite morality.

In such groups there would be no sense of history and no grandiose ambitions for a future life. Hunter-gatherers may have been consummate campsite problem solvers, but they were not reflective about matters of human nature, origins, and destiny. Nor would they have felt a sense of group identity. The group itself was not recognized as an entity. They achieved solidarity and cohesiveness, for sure, but these grew out of personal attachments between individuals rather than any sense of belonging to a transcendent whole. Moral obligations were determined by reciprocity and emotional exigency—you shared everything with everyone, either because you felt affection, sympathy, or gratitude toward them, or because you feared reprisals. Immediate gut feelings were sufficient, so there was no need to formulate explicit rules of moral conduct. The behavioral algorithms underlying this implicit morality appear to be designed to regulate social order on a very small scale, for whenever groups grew beyond a certain size the algorithms would falter and overlaps of self-interest would degenerate into conflicts of interest, eventually resulting in social fission. This was the standard pattern of social organization among our ancestors: growth-fission-growth-fission-growth . . .

It was not until the great leap forward, no more than fifty thousand years ago, that humans managed to break the cycle of growth and fission to begin living harmoniously in larger groups. The advantages inherent in larger-scale social organization would have been real. A larger group would mean greater productivity, enabling the buildup of food surpluses to hedge against temporary shortages. Larger groups could tackle larger prey with predictable success. They would be less vulnerable to raids by other groups, and more capable of executing their own raids. And, importantly, larger groups would have an expanded knowledge base. In short, a larger group would assure greater prosperity and security. The real puzzle is not why our ancestors started forming larger groups at the time of the great leap forward, but why they failed to do so much earlier. What was the obstacle to larger-scale social organization?

Social systems are just like other systems in at least one respect: the more components in the system, the more complex the rules must be for coordinating them in an orderly manner. Consider a simple game of catch between two players, Peter and Paul. This is a two-particle system having very simple rules. Peter follows the rule, "catch ball from Paul, then throw ball to Paul." Paul follows his own version of the same rule. Suppose, now, that Mary enters the game. It will still be a game of catch, but the addition of a third player necessarily complicates the rules. When Peter catches the ball he must now have a rule to determine whether to throw it to Paul or Mary. Keeping the game orderly requires more complex rules. One thing is clear, however: if Peter and Paul continue playing by the old rules the three-particle system will collapse. Mary will get upset at being excluded and will probably pack off—or worse, she may vent her anger at Peter and Paul.

Early attempts at large group living would have been faced with a similar challenge. For thousands of generations the game of sociality had followed the rules of emotional gut reactions. This implicit morality mandated the campsite scale of social organization. If hunting-gathering groups managed to increase substantially in size during boom periods, social relations were sure to become strained, making fission into independent subgroups likely. Any experiment in larger-group living would have to introduce new rules for behavior that were appropriate to the new scale of sociality. But what were the rules for maintaining harmony in a large group? No one would have known, of course. But more seriously, the very idea of having rules to regulate social behavior would have felt strange to hunter-gatherers. It is not that the social order of the campsite was unregulated, but that the regulation was implicit, automatically enforced at a preconscious level by inherited algorithms. To acquire new rules for enlarged group life would require one of two things: either a fortuitous mutation in the algorithms underlying the old morality, or the ad hoc invention of explicit rules to override the sirens of implicit morality. What happened, of course, was the latter. But, again, what were the appropriate ad hoc rules that needed to be imposed? And furthermore, what could possibly induce individuals accustomed to a life of instant gratification to comply with them?

We may suppose that our ancestors engaged in many failed attempts to pass through the bottleneck from implicit morality to explicit morality. To describe how they made this breakthrough is a bit like describing how biological systems emerged from chemical systems: there are many plausible ways in which it *might* have happened. I propose the following.

In the course of their migrations hunting-gathering bands would inevitably encounter other small groups, perhaps at watering holes where large fauna swarmed. Encounters such as this, where there was more than enough game for everyone, would tend to be friendly. They might even be exhilarating and memorable. In addition, individuals might spontaneously cooperate in the kill, perhaps learning a thing or two, and sharing a meal together. Such meetings might even result in the exchange of a few females. One can only guess at the duration of such events, but it is likely that tensions would eventually swell to a flash point and outbreaks of hostility would end the party as quickly as it began. Lacking the social means for resolving conflicts on this larger scale, groups would be relieved to part company with good riddance. How often would events like this occur during the lifetime of an individual? Impossible to say, of course, but one might safely assume that the probability of such chance occurrences would vary with ecological fluctuations. One can easily imagine circumstances under which a few small bands might begin to regularize such meetings by reuniting on a seasonal basis. Doing so would constitute a major advance in social organization.

Periodic reunions must have been common during the millennia before the great leap forward. It was probably not unusual for coalitions of this sort to be ended once and for all by the demise of one of the groups. And presumably an exceptionally ugly incident during the course of a reunion might result in two groups remaining permanent enemies, each of them careful to avoid returning to the scene. But what would follow from a pattern in which two groups reunite each year for several years running? During the months of separation individuals in each group would reflect on the previous reunion and anticipate the next one. They might even prepare for it by making special gifts. When reunions took place the tempo of social life would rev up to a bazaar-like pitch as the groups feasted together, exchanged gifts, and selected mating partners. In time, the reunion events would become stereotyped as participants would know what activities to expect and when. A series of simple rituals might begin to develop. The annual exchange of members (especially females) would eventually result in a shared language and a shared cosmology, not to mention the genetic ties. Lots of personal information would be exchanged, including accounts of what had become of nonreturning participants. A good share of time spent in reunion events would be devoted to stories and fond recollections of reunions past. In the end, however, the atmosphere of these events would thicken with stress and restlessness, and everyone would be happy to return to the more comfortable scale of meandering camp life.

Allowing for these kinds of encounters enables the following points. First, the formation of episodic yet stable coalitions between hunting-gathering groups may have been the most radical social transformation ever in the history of our species, preparing the foundations for subsequent transformations to tribal alliances, chiefdoms, nation states, and (perhaps even) a global federation. Each of these transformations may be described in the language of emergent systems. The change from the intuitive sociality of hunting-gathering bands to episodic coalitions is analogous to the emergence of multicellularity from unicellular life forms. Also, it is striking to realize how quickly such a transformation might occur, and how quickly it might be lost to the default sociality.

Secondly, episodic coalitions of hunting-gathering bands offered the best of both worlds to our Paleolithic ancestors. For one thing, the external support provided a measure of prosperity and security that isolated hunter-gatherers could not achieve. But at the same time, these coalitions were minimally demanding in terms of individual investment and sacrifice. When the costs of social investment escalated there was always the exit option, yet when you needed help there was somewhere to go.

Thirdly, the formation of episodic coalitions would call for the invention and enforcement of explicit rules for behavior. A more complex social order requires more complex rules for maintaining it. We all know that certain behaviors tolerated at home with the family are often not allowed in public. When you're at church or at Grandma's house you're expected to be on your best behavior. The same discrepancy would have held between normal camp life and the more complex social context of reunion events—only worse, for it would have felt like an absolute difference between rules and no rules. The intuitive morality of camp life came naturally, there were no explicit rules to learn and to obey because moral conduct was governed by gut reactions. But reunion life was unnatural, counterintuitive. In the reunion context there were things you could not do, no matter how intensely you felt like doing them. And there were things you had to do, despite your inclination to refuse. In the reunion context everyone had to exercise a lot more deliberate control over their behavior, and this would have been very difficult and stressful for individuals accustomed to a life of instant gratification. Nevertheless, they somehow managed . . . more or less.

There is no way to determine the nature of the first articulate morality, but we may be confident that the specific rules were generated by the following algorithm: *thou shalt not do whatever it was that caused trouble at the last reunion*. This would be an excellent general strategy for kick-starting formal morality, but the simplicity of this algorithm is deceptive. For one thing, it would not always be clear exactly what caused trouble at the last reunion. Maybe it was *this* behavior, but then it could have been *that* one. To be on the safe side there should perhaps be rules against both behaviors. Furthermore, we can be sure that different behaviors caused trouble in different years. Thus, we can easily see how this general algorithm, simple as it appears, could begin to generate a rather elaborate set of explicit rules. Each year, therefore, the psychological costs of reunion life would escalate. But the upside would be that if the right rules were introduced then each year the reunion event would be more satisfying and harmonious.

Here it must be noted that the introduction of ad hoc moral rules would have a decisive bearing on the dynamics of self-conception and self-monitoring. To learn explicit rules for behavior is to acquire performance standards for an ideal self against which individuals compare their actual behaviors in a process of self-monitoring. During reunion events individuals would be engaged in a radically new way of thinking about themselves.

And finally, the formation of episodic coalitions would have generated a sense of group identity. Isolated bands were identifiable groups too, but individuals would hardly be aware of this fact. The camp group was a mere epiphenomenon, a negligible byproduct of the real substance of sociality, which was all about personal attachments. But the discrepancy between the atomic life of the band and the molecular life of the coalition would have made "grouphood" a salient social fact, no longer to be taken for granted. One now entered into a group in a deliberate manner, and on the inside everything would feel strange. The group was suddenly a *thing*, an entity that one might think about, a reality about which one might bear an attitude, a presence to which one seems to be obligated. Yet finding a satisfying way to think about the molecular group would be extraordinarily difficult. One could not actually *see* this mysterious entity, although its reality could not be denied. What *kind* of reality is it?

From our point of view it was an emergent reality. Our ancestors got into large-scale sociality in a small way at first—on a part-time experimental basis—and we cannot assume that the results were uniformly positive. It is probable that some episodic coalitions failed due to environmental factors, some due to disease, and in other cases the experiment might have failed because of poor insights about which rules to enforce, or because the means of enforcement were too harsh. But eventually the enterprise stabilized and progressive cultural traditions emerged.

We will fail to understand the depth of this social transformation if we do not appreciate how the sheer novelty of it generated a crisis of self-understanding. I have suggested that the introduction of explicit rules triggered changes in the way individuals thought about themselves and their groups. Ultimately this would have been the case, but initially it is probably more accurate to say that it triggered confusion and perplexity. At the very least, the new social circumstances would have generated both ambivalence and dissonance in the minds of individuals—ambivalence because the larger group was both freeing and limiting, both exhilarating and frustrating; and dissonance because the movement between social contexts would burden individuals with potential for internally conflicting values. Ambivalence and dissonance are threats to personal wholeness, and individuals experiencing these states would hunger for the means to resolve them.

The deep point is that the new experiment in postintuitive sociality would have left individuals confused and perplexed about fundamental personal and social realities. We may summarize the crisis of self-understanding in the following set of questions:

> What kind of reality is a human being?
> What is good for a human being?
> What kind of reality is a social group?
> What is good for the social order?

Obviously, the questions would not have appeared in anything like these precise forms, but these were nevertheless the pressing concerns. And these are precisely the pressing concerns of every counterintuitively large social entity. When we took the great leap forward we brought upon ourselves an entirely new universe of meanings.

Why do I claim that the transition to large-scale sociality represents a strong emergent phenomenon? I do so because I believe that counterintuitively large social groups are real entities with novel properties calling for the formulation of additional laws of nature. Margaret Thatcher was dead wrong when she once famously said, "Society does not exist, only households exist." Emergence is about new realities, but that does not mean that some new kind of stuff enters the picture. The only thing that enters the picture is new relationships between components that are already there. When existing parts enter into new dynamical relations then the possibilities exist for new realities to emerge.

And why do I claim that the emergence of a new social reality involved a transformation of human nature? The great leap forward was enabled by unprecedented and irreversible dynamics of self-consciousness in the form of self-monitoring and group identity. Suddenly, human existence—both personal and collective—became problematic in ways that were previously inconceivable. Questioning the meaning of life, once utterly unthinkable, now became inevitable, but it also became an essential part of the human strategy for pursuing personal wholeness and social coherence. To have explicit *concepts* for these goals—to have a sense of the self as a moral agent and a sense of one's group as a transcendent entity—changed everything about the way humans perceived possibilities for a full and responsible existence. Seeking personal wholeness and social coherence would now take the form of a *project*. No other species pursues the twin telē on even remotely comparable terms. Humans are the only species to pursue a meaningful existence by questioning the meaning of existence.

I have speculated that the great leap forward followed a crisis of self-understanding. The pressing concerns had to be addressed. If there were no satisfying ways to think about the nature and the nurture of the self and the social order, then someone would have to come up with some ideas. If the emergent realities were left unexplained, and if the explicit moral order was not justified, then the great experiment in postintuitive sociality would remain inherently unstable. In this way the crisis of self-understanding gave birth to wisdom traditions, that is, narrative accounts of who we are, where we came from, and what we are for. The point of a wisdom tradition is to show us that the relation between the twin telē of personality and sociality does not necessarily amount to an either-or proposition—that is, these goals can be achieved simultaneously. In other words, the point of wisdom traditions is to broker the marriage of happiness and virtue. It is now part of our emergent human nature to create such traditions as the means to our salvation.

Inventionism

This chapter set out to develop an emergence perspective on meaning in a manner that incorporates certain elements from inherentist, inventionist, and reductionist perspectives. What we have at the moment looks rather like a robust version of inherentism without the cosmic topping—that is, there may be no telē woven into the ultimate fabric of reality, but there are purposes embedded in the adaptive strategies of living organisms. All living things have it in their nature to seek the ultimate goal of viability, each according to its inherent strategies. Many living things have it in their nature to seek the ultimate goal by means of the penultimate values of individual integrity and collective cohesiveness. But human beings alone have it in their nature to create symbolic cultural traditions, including wisdom traditions, for the sake of achieving these penultimate values. It might appear that this perspective locates far too much meaning in the world to be compatible with inventionism. But let's see.

Inventionism, recall, takes the view that all meanings are contingent upon particular psychological dynamics or particular social dynamics. All purposes are historical, contextual, and concrete. Inventionists are especially keen to abolish essentialist thinking about what human beings are for. There is no universal human nature, they insist. Humans are for whatever they (in their uniqueness) invent for themselves, either by subjective imagination or by social negotiation. References to abstract and objective telē are firmly rejected. There is no all-purpose purpose, either for individuals or for cultural traditions. Meaning is local, not global. Inventionists will find reason to object to the present state of the emergence perspective on two fronts. I will call these "the human objection" and "the biological objection."

The human objection might go something like this. Viability is an empty abstraction. Personal wholeness and social coherence are empty abstractions too. Even if we (inventionists) were to recognize these goals, we would insist that nobody achieves viability in general, and nobody achieves personal integrity or social solidarity in general either. The *means* to these abstract ends are necessarily relative to particular psychological and social circumstances. As for wisdom: there is no generalized wisdom tradition, any more than there is language in general. Just as there are many particular ways to be a living thing, there are many particular ways to be whole persons and coherent societies. If one is to become a whole person, then he or she must do it in a radically *specific* way, and all specific ways are relative. The same goes for social coherence: the solidarity of a group is always a matter of overcoming highly specific challenges. And besides, who gets to say what counts as "whole" and "coherent"? To say that human beings are *for* personal wholeness and social coherence is to say nothing—it is like going into a restaurant and ordering food in general.

It strikes me that the substance of this line of reasoning might be construed in terms of weak or strong forms of inventionism. In its weak form, inventionism amounts to a frontal attack on all forms of essentialist thinking. It is true that there are many particular ways to be a whole person and many particular ways to organize social groups. There are many incommensurable ways to construct wisdom traditions as well. And many ways to pursue the marriage of happiness and virtue. I concede that the inventionist argument for particularity and diversity in approaching concrete meaning-of-life questions is indefeasible. And what this means is that particular, *proximate* purposes are *not* objectively in the world. If inherentism tries to get specific it degenerates into essentialism. It is reasonable to expect, therefore, that emergentists will have no serious objections to a weak form of inventionism.

Strong inventionism, however, is a different matter. The strong inventionist perspective would reject notions such as personal wholeness and social coherence as culturally relative and socially constructed abstractions having no universal application. If there is no universal human nature, then there is no universally acceptable way to bring substance to concepts such as personality and sociality. For strong inventionists, any generalized observations about human beings amounts to essentialism. And if I have this right, strong inventionism implies that there would be nothing contrary to human nature in actions that deliberately undermined what our emergence account loosely defined as personal wholeness and social coherence. This is not the place to undertake an exhaustive critique of extreme inventionism. That job has been well and thoroughly performed in Steven Pinker's 2002 book, *The Blank Slate*.[5] I take it as well settled that the strong inventionist rejection of human nature (statistically and temporally defined) is intellectually moribund.

Richard Rorty has objected to the idea that personal goals for self-creation might be unified with social goals for solidarity and cooperation. I take this to be a strong inventionist rejection of the possibilities for constructing coherent wisdom traditions. I have suggested that wisdom traditions have been developed for the sake of helping us to make large-scale social organization into a non-zero-sum game. In other words, they help us to see that self-creation is not necessarily incompatible with social harmony—in fact, these goals are mutually reinforcing. Rorty, however, believes that all attempts at this sort of "wisdom" have failed, and that the project itself ought to be given up.[6] That is to say, the marriage of happiness and virtue is a lost cause. I confess that I have little to say in response to Rorty's objection. My impression is that his expectations for the success of wisdom traditions were set a bit too high. Utopia has not been achieved, so why bother? One can agree with Rorty that individuals are often caught up in zero-sum relations with their social environs without agreeing that wisdom traditions can do nothing to improve the situation. The judgment that these traditions have proven to be universal failures is unsubstantiated, and a willingness to abandon completely the quest for wisdom strikes me as a failure of courage and hope.

The biological objection might go something like the following. Adaptive traits are historical artifacts. They are there in the world, scripted in genetic code, providing goal direction to the organisms that have them. But these telē bear no objective relation to present circumstances in the world. They are contingent on the past circumstances of natural selection, relative to particular historical contexts. To say that particular traits have been adaptive in the past tells us nothing significant about their fitness for the present or the future. Traits that have proven themselves adaptive in one context often turn out to be maladaptive when the context changes. With respect to the future these telē are akin to inventions, mere speculations, guesswork. They are imaginative stabs in the dark, and as such they are not reliable guides to a meaningful life.

The observation that adaptive traits are historically contingent artifacts is true, of course, and it bears heavily against any strong form of inherentism that drifts toward biological essentialism. But the observation does not bear against a reformed version of inherentism, one that insists on the temporal and statistical character of species traits. And the observation hardly provokes anxiety among emergentists, who give way to no one when it comes to the unpredictability of future events. Adaptive traits are clearly "inventions" of a blind process, and they are clearly relative to historical circumstances. But to suggest that they are therefore irrelevant to the future takes the argument to the point of absurdity. The dynamics of life work with probabilities, and while there are no guarantees of adaptivity in the future there are irresistibly strong odds that what has worked in the past will continue to do so in the foreseeable future. The claim that there are telē embodied in our traits (and therefore in the world) is nearly an obvious truth, and the relevance of these telē for apprehending the ultimate and penultimate goals of human life is nearly undeniable.

At the risk of belaboring the obvious, I will add one further note of clarification. I have been advocating an alliance of emergentism with inherentism by claiming that the ultimate goal of viability and the penultimate goals of personal wholeness and social coherence are inherent in human nature. At the same time, however, I have advocated an alliance with inventionism by insisting that proximate goals and values—the ones we tend to argue about on a daily basis— are *not* inherent in our nature. These immediate goals and values are constructs of subjective imagination and social negotiation, and are therefore relative, contingent, contextual, and optional.

Interlude: A Model of Emergence

At this point the argument of the chapter will be put on hold while we briefly examine a speculative model for the emergence of life proposed by Terrence Deacon. You may recall the point made several pages ago that the process of evolution by natural selection assumes the concept of function—that is, evolutionary theory explains how life develops, but it says nothing about the origins of living, functional systems. The perspective that has been developing in this chapter holds that teleology (*so that* causal influence) is an emergent property of living systems. This gave us the paradoxical claim that purposeful biological behaviors spontaneously emerged from the pointless meanderings of a nonliving cosmos. The principal opponents of this view are inherentists (who insist that telē must be inherent in the world from the beginning), and reductionists (who insist on the reducibility of *so that* causes to *because of* causes). The burden for emergentism is to show how teleology amounts to a radically new and irreducibly real phenomenon in the natural world. This is no slight burden, since it amounts to producing a principled account of the origins of life—that is, showing how the properties of living organisms might have resulted from novel relationships between nonliving components. We need to be clear about one point: the burden on the emergence theorist is not actually to *create* living systems, but rather to provide a plausible theoretical scenario for their creation without making any controversial assumptions.

The biological anthropologist and neuroscientist Terrence Deacon has worked out a hypothetical account of how teleological phenomena might have emerged from the straightforward causal dynamics known to physics and chemistry. This model provides a theoretical link between non-life and life. Many origin-of-life investigators work on the assumption that the key thing to be explained is the origin of complex information molecules (RNA, DNA) that specify the shapes of self-organizing structures. Others, including Deacon, see the process working the other way around: complex self-organizing structures appeared first, and the informational piece of the puzzle came into play later.

We begin by recalling the basic principle of emergence: when components in a system are brought into new dynamical relations with each other, probabilities increase for the spontaneous emergence of new properties. This principle is at work everywhere in nature. With this principle in mind, Deacon recognizes three types of emergent phenomena. The first involves the emergence of new properties resulting from *thermodynamic effects*. The water example will again help us with this. We recognize that water has several properties, including viscosity (liquid state), hardness (ice), buoyancy (ice), and surface tension (liquid). Individual molecules of H_2O have none of these properties, but when H_2O molecules are brought into particular relationships the new properties emerge spontaneously. The second type results from *morphodynamic effects*. Here we see a process in which forms, or patterns, interact in ways that generate emergent forms or patterns. In other words, in addition to the influence of energy dynamics, it is important to recognize that shapes have influence in the form of imposing constraints, an important contributing factor in the causal story. Morphodynamic effects emerge when these constraints operate as decisive factors in the generation of new shapes and in executing functions based on emergent shapes. The snowflake, for example, arises as a consequence of morphodynamics. Here again, nothing is present but water molecules, but the peculiar shape taken by an initial ice crystal provides a crucial shape bias that self-amplifies into a uniquely complex geometrical pattern. The idea that shapes have decisive constraining properties is central to the Deacon model. There is no question of thermodynamic effects falling out of the picture, or being overpowered by the influence of shapes. Thermodynamic effects continue to rule, always, but shapes can exert critical influences in addition to thermodynamic effects. The third type of emergent phenomena is associated with *teleodynamic effects*, or goal-directed behaviors, of which the activities of a bacterium and your reading of this book are excellent examples.

So far, so good. Now, the question that Deacon set out to answer was this: How might pointless thermodynamic and morphodynamic effects give rise to purposeful teleodynamic effects? The short answer is this: just as thermodynamic considerations are preconditions for the emergence of morphodynamic effects, so also may novel relationships among morphodynamic emergents lead to teleodynamic effects.[7] In other words, the pathway from pointlessness to purpose is mediated by the intervention of morphodynamic effects and natural selection. The full story centers on Deacon's model of the *autocell*, a theoretical construct of an emergent entity that displays some of the properties of living systems.

The autocell is a relatively simple molecular structure generated by a reciprocal relationship between two self-organizing processes: an *autocatalytic cycle* and a *self-assembling capsule*, or container. Catalysts are molecular agents that influence the rates of chemical reactions. Autocatalysis is a phenomenon whereby a few different catalysts (a set) get together and rev themselves up into an autocatalytic cycle. Each catalyst in the set contributes to the production of another member of the set, which contributes to another, and so on, until we get a self-perpetuating and self-amplifying cyclical process (the ultimate non-zero-sum game in which every catalyst is a big winner).

The spontaneous self-assembly of container-like structures (little tubes or globes) is a common morphodynamic process (virus shells, for example). Imagine a cloud of material substrates—tiny molecules with sticky properties—bumping into each other accidentally in a chemically rich environment. When these molecular shapes collide with each other, some may tend to stick together, forming architecturally impressive aggregates (form begetting form). See Figure 3.1 for an illustration of the process.

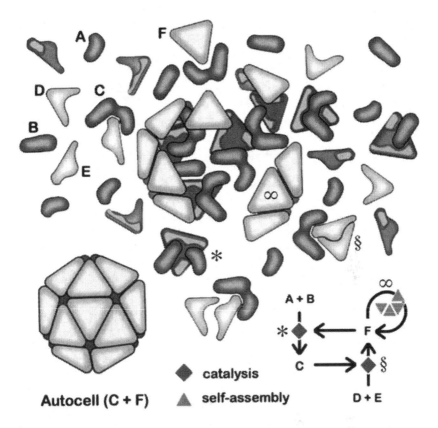

Figure 3.1. This image depicts the dynamics of autocell assembly based on a minimal number of catalytic components. Component molecules have distinct geometrical properties that determine their interactions. A, B, D, and E represent "primordial soup" substrate molecules, assumed to pre-exist in the surrounding medium. C and F represent synthesized catalysts produced from bonded substrates. The letter and arrow diagram (lower right) schematizes the process of autocell assembly. [From Deacon (2006), used with permission.]

When you link autocatalytic cycling together with self-assembling containers in a reciprocal relationship you get an autocell. Here's how the reciprocity goes. Autocatalytic cycles help out the container-building process because the building blocks for the containers are generated by the cycles. So autocatalysis assures a healthy supply of container parts. And the containers help out the autocatalysis by preventing members of the set from floating away, thus assuring a continuation of the cycle of chemical composition. The probability of each process is increased by the other. That is, containers are more likely to self-assemble in the vicinity of catalysts that manufacture their components, and the manufacture of these components is more likely when members of the manufacturing workforce are prevented from leaving the premises.

Autocells are posited to be unstable in the sense that they occasionally break open to the environment when perturbed, and then reassemble themselves. This allows substrates to enter and drive new rounds of the cycle, which otherwise stops when substrates are exhausted. It also offers the possibility for new types of material substrates to enter the structure. New substrates create the potential for initiating different and more complex autocatalytic cycles. The cycle of breakup and reassembly is likely to result in differential efficiencies among autocell designs, such that more efficient forms would be more plentiful. Here we begin to see, in rudimentary forms, some of the features of living systems: self-replication, exploitation of substrates, and evolvability by natural selection. One may even say that the property of functioning is minimally present—that is, relative to autocells *as entities*, autocatalysis and assembly/repair are *activities performed by the autocells* that result in their persistence.

Autocells are not living systems—they lack separate encoding systems characteristic of all earthly life forms—but neither are they mere playthings of their environment. Each autocell is destined to break up, but if the environment is sufficiently tranquil they will spontaneously reassemble themselves, only to break up again and reassemble. Under these circumstances, occasional iterations in the process may be more complex than previous ones, introducing the prospect of a ratchet effect of increasing chemical complexity. An example of increased complexity might involve a subset of molecules able to store up energy, an innovation that would allow the autocell to carry on even when fresh energizing substrates are in short supply. This would increase the autocell's independence from the immediate environment. It is also possible—without making any further assumptions—for autocells to develop submechanisms that would facilitate the entry of particular substrates or block the entry of others. Eventually, then, the most abundant autocells would be the ones having traits for admitting "nutrients" and blocking "toxins." In addition, reassembly events might accidentally capture large molecules that are good at encoding, which might equip an autocell with new ways to specify the shapes of its catalysts and containers. Such mechanisms would give an autocell a new form of independence from the chance offerings of the environment. Autocells equipped with any of these mechanisms would outcompete autocells without them.

An autocell is an autocatalytic structure fully capable, even in its simplest form, of incorporating additional submechanisms that might contribute to its original property of self-maintenance. To repeat a centrally important point: autocells are *evolvable*. Consider an autocell that grows incrementally ever more complex by incorporating interdependent subsystems. If each increment has the effect of making autocell reiteration more probable, then at some point we're going to suspect that autocells do the things they do *so that* they might persist in doing them. That is, at some point it becomes difficult to resist the conclusion that telē (and agency) have emerged. There is no sharp line that divides life from non-life, but the autocell model gives us all the theoretical license we need to suspect that the fuzzy line tells a story about the probability enhancements of morphodynamics processes. Emergent forms increase probabilities for additional emergent forms, a process that makes possible the emergence of genuine functions.

The Miracle of Meaning

Every human culture we are aware of has had its own distinctive narrative about the nature of reality and the place of human life in the grand scheme of things. When human beings, for whatever reasons, raise questions about the meaning of life, they are inviting answers on the largest scale of all. They want to know the final, inside story about how things ultimately are in the cosmos, and they want to know which values are ultimately true. To know these things is to have our bearings in nature and in history.

We human beings of the twenty-first century have come to a point of sophistication where we can say with rare certainty (though not always with enthusiasm) that we shall never have these final truths that we feel so intensely entitled to. And yet, for the very first time in the history of our species, we have before us an astonishing and captivating narrative that has the unique power to unite all of humanity in a common vision. And we can say, again with rare certainty, that it is also the truest comprehensive narrative ever told. I mean, of course, the grand narrative of the evolution of matter, life, and mind. Elements of this narrative have been unfolding before us since the dawn of modern science in the seventeenth century, but the story has become especially broad, deep and sharp during the course of the past century.

There are, however, two problems with this narrative: a minor one and a major one. The minor problem is that this is not a final story. We know that there is much more to come, and we have good reason to believe that parts of the story will undergo revision. But we can tolerate this incompleteness because we know we're on the right course, and we know it's the best story so far told—which is all we can now expect "final" to mean.

The major difficulty with the grand narrative of cosmic evolution is that it tells only half the story: it is descriptive but not prescriptive. That is, the story informs us about the age, the history and the workings of the universe, but it falls silent on matters of value and meaning. Unlike the grand narratives of ancient cultures, our story brings no interpretive material embedded within it, leaving us on our own to decide what to make of it. And this accounts for the centrality of questions of meaning throughout the modern era, as well as the existential urgency we attach to them.

Meaning is a teleological concept, and any discussion of it inevitably leads us to ask about the prospects for apprehending the ultimate purpose of our lives. In this chapter and the previous one we have been exploring questions about the reality of purposeful phenomena. I have suggested that efforts to come to terms with these phenomena have generated three major perspectives. Inherentism is the general view that purposes are inherent in the world. Inventionism rejects the metaphysical flavor of inherentism and locates purposes in the contexts of subjective imagination and social negotiation. Reductionism takes the view that purposeful behavior is a mere illusion, insisting on the reducibility of *so that* dynamics to *because of* dynamics. The message of the present chapter is that, whereas these familiar perspectives offer useful insights, we now have a more satisfying way to think about the reality of purpose and meaning: the emergence option.

Emergentism can be broadly understood against the backdrop of ancient approaches to nature. Ancient philosophers used concepts of substance, process, and form to explain natural phenomena. Most started with an idea of substance (e.g., water) and then proceeded to describe the processes by which the primary substance undergoes transformations. Some started with the ultimacy of form, while others placed the emphasis on process. Emergentism offers a distinctive alternative in its emphasis on factors such as reciprocal relationships, shape changes, amplification effects, and the bearing these have on probabilities for genuine novelty in the universe.

Like all close observers of nature, emergentists have been impressed by its hierarchical processes and structures. The human body, for example, reveals hierarchical processes, where higher-level functions emerge from lower-level functions. The biotic world itself is hierarchically organized, usually from smaller and simpler organisms to larger and more complex species. Everywhere we look in nature we find levels of organization. Contemporary emergentists, inspired by Big Bang cosmology, associate the hierarchical structures of the natural order with its historical development: simplicity of organization is *lower* than complexity because it is typically *earlier*. In all these respects it is evident that contemporary science embodies at least a weak emergence perspective on nature. It is only when it comes to explaining the details of emergent phenomena that we find the distinction arise between a strong form of emergentism, on one hand, and reductionism, on the other.

In this chapter I have sketched out a view of teleological phenomena within the context of an emergentist perspective. There is no official emergence position on the question of meaning, and I expect that most emergentists would throw a fit if I were to suggest that the view presented here represents *the* emergence doctrine on teleology. For one thing, I have approached the question of purposeful phenomena on the assumption of both naturalist and materialist principles, and it is by no means clear that these metaphysical commitments are implicit in emergentism. The picture that has been developing here represents what may be no more than a minority opinion among emergentists.

I have tried to make it clear how the view I have espoused on meaning is consistent with, yet divergent from, certain elements in the inherentist, inventionist, and reductionist perspectives. Having confessed to a pro-reductionist bias, I have agreed that there are no good reasons to believe that the universe has any inherent purposes among its fundamental attributes, and no good reasons to believe that purposes have been assigned to the universe by a transcendent source. The apprehension of telos at the level of cosmic principles is most probably an illusion. In contrast to the strong reductionist view, however, I believe there are good reasons to claim that genuine purposefulness is a real and emergent property of living systems. Living things act in such ways that their behavior cannot be rendered fully intelligible without substantial supplements to the explanatory principles of physics and chemistry. Teleodynamics are real.

In sympathy with inherentism, I have agreed that meaning is inherent in the objective world by virtue of the various telē found embodied in the heritable traits of living organisms. The inherent nature of these telē, I argued, justifies the claim that certain values are objectively true. All species of living things, for example, have it in their nature to seek the ultimate goal of reproductive fitness (viability), and all attempts to explain or to justify the behavior of living things apart from this goal will be incomplete. In addition, many species (including humans) have it objectively in their nature to seek the penultimate goals of individual integrity and social harmony. Humans, I maintained, are unique in pursuing these penultimate goals by means of emergent, progressive cultural traditions.

In sympathy with inventionism I readily agreed that essentialist categories are indefensible, which implies that no adaptive species traits (inherent telē) are absolute or eternal. But in contrast to extreme inventionists I have argued that a blanket rejection of human nature is unjustified and dogmatic. The concept of an objective human nature is both coherent and verifiable, so long as one is equipped with a species concept that is statistically and temporally defined. Also in sympathy with inventionism, I agreed that all but the most generalized values are relative to psychological and social variables, which implies that there are no fixed proximate goals inherent in our human nature. And finally, in contrast to some versions of postmodern inventionsim, I have defended the view that it is possible to achieve a consistent vision of a meaningful life that places subjective desires in harmony with public virtues.

And what, finally, does all of this yield for our inquiry into the meaning of life? Very briefly, if you want to have a genuinely meaningful life you must:

stay alive (duh!)
commit yourself to the active pursuit of goals that are simul-
    taneously personally satisfying and socially constructive

All that remains is to use your imagination.

All that remains for this chapter is to construct a bridge to the topic of religious naturalism. This will be relatively simple because I have come to the view that strong emergentism quite naturally calls for a religious response. And I take this view because I believe that the emerging universe is a miraculous event.

I will have to be careful here because talk of miracles typically conjures up images of pixie dust and magic wands. By "miracle" I do not mean an impossible event taking place at the behest of a supernatural agent. I mean only this: any event, the occurrence of which is so radically improbable as to be completely unbelievable. I am excluding logically impossible events from the discussion because they have a probability of zero. Even gods cannot square a circle. A miracle is an event having a probability value so close to zero that you cannot imagine its occurrence. That said, I think it is nearly obvious that miracles happen *all the time* in our universe—it's just that they never happen *before their time*. But consider what happens to probabilities in the emerging universe. They change!

Put yourself backward in time to some point immediately after the Big Bang, when the universe was nothing but a raging inferno (no quarks, no atoms, just pure energy). If someone were to suggest to you that nearly fifteen billion years hence you would be sitting there reading a book you would be completely incredulous. The probabilities against such an event happening would be incalculable. But there you are. And you got there, not because of some magic wand, but because of the countless number of probability-enhancing events that have intervened between the Big Bang and today. The cumulative effect of these events has produced a miracle.

Now put yourself back to four billion years ago. At that point you would be, again, completely incredulous if someone were to predict that in a short while there would be living organisms on the young planet Earth able to act with purpose and meaning. You couldn't manage such a thought four billion years ago because "acting with purpose" and "having meaning" were not properties that existed anywhere in the known universe. But they are now, and they emerged spontaneously from an absurd, meaningless coincidence of events. Miracles happen all the time in our universe, but never before their time.

We have the lives we do because they were made incrementally less improbable by the epic events of cosmic evolution, whereby matter was "distilled out of radiant energy, segregated into galaxies, collapsed into stars, fused into atoms, swirled into planets, spliced into molecules, captured into cells, mutated into species, compromised into ecosystems, provoked into thought, and cajoled into cultures."[8] Does such a universe invite a religious response, or what?

PART TWO

RELIGIOUS NATURALISM

Introduction

Part One of this book examined four distinct perspectives on the reality of teleological phenomena. There I tried to show that the emergence perspective overlaps in some important ways with inherentism, inventionism, and reductionism, yet avoids their most serious problems.

The question before us in the remaining two chapters is whether the emergence perspective provides an adequate platform for constructing a plausible naturalistic vision of the religious life. Chapter 4 begins with a naturalized account of religious phenomena, and then describes some of the salient features of religious naturalism. The discussion then moves to a defense of religious naturalism against charges that it is intellectually and spiritually deficient. Chapter 5 attempts to show how some familiar religious themes take on new meanings when considered from the perspective of a religious naturalist.

4

Religion Naturalized, Nature Sanctified

The first thing to say about the term *religious naturalism* is that it is not an oxymoron. Of course, it *would* be an oxymoron if "religion" were understood to imply belief in supernatural entities and events, or if "naturalism" were defined in terms of an aversion to religious sensibilities. But it is precisely these misunderstandings that religious naturalists are eager to address. Naturalism is, roughly speaking, the view that the order of nature is all that exists. If something is real it is natural, and if something is natural it is real. This way of thinking does away with the belief that outside of nature (or prior to nature) there exists another, more ultimately real and good, supernatural order. The naturalist believes that outside of nature, or prior to nature, there is nothing meaningful to talk about. If God exists, then God is a natural being, or a natural process, or nature itself. Religious naturalists are, first and foremost, naturalists.

The question remains whether naturalists can be, in any coherent sense, religious. Many naturalists—perhaps most of them—would reject any sort of identification with religion, and even religious naturalists will take pains to disavow their association with most of what passes under the name of religion. But this does not mean that naturalists cannot be genuinely religious. If we mean by "religious" a set of attitudes and sensibilities (rather than a set of metaphysical doctrines or an institutional allegiance), then we might bring ourselves to accept the fact that some people find their intellectual and emotional responses to the natural world to be recognizably religious. A religious naturalist, then, is a naturalist who is, or seeks to be, religiously engaged with the natural order. With this brief definition in place we may proceed to the details.

Bringing Religion Down to Earth

Here is the prophet Isaiah commenting on the religious behavior of his neighbors:

> A man plants a cedar and the rain makes it grow, so that later on he will have cedars to cut down; or he chooses an ilex or an oak to raise a stout tree for himself in the forest. It becomes fuel for his fire: some of it he takes and warms himself, some he kindles and bakes bread on it, and some he makes into a god and prostrates himself, shaping it into an idol and bowing down before it. The one half of it he burns in the fire and on this he roasts meat, so that he may eat his roast and be satisfied; he also warms himself at it and he says, "Good! I can feel the heat, I am growing warm." Then what is left of the wood he makes into a god by carving it into shape; he bows down to it and prostrates himself and prays to it, saying, "Save me; for thou are my god." Such people neither know nor understand, their eyes made too blind to see, their minds too narrow to discern. Such a man will not use his reason, he has neither the wit nor the sense to say, "Half of it I have burnt, yes, and used its embers to bake bread; I have roasted the meat on them too and eaten it; but the rest of it I turn into this abominable thing and so I am worshipping a log of wood." He feeds on ashes indeed! His own deluded mind has misled him, he cannot recollect himself so far as to say, "Why! This thing in my hand is a sham."[1]

In this passage we see Isaiah bringing the religion of his neighbors down to earth. He is engaged in the business of naturalizing religion, that is, showing that the best explanation for religious beliefs and practices is a natural one, not the presumed supernatural one. He's being a good reductionist by showing that what his neighbors *think* they're doing is in fact not what they're *really* doing. His only mistake, of course, is that he didn't finish the job. For if he had, he would have given his own religious behavior a similar treatment.

To naturalize some phenomenon is just to show that it can in principle be explained by natural causes. For example, various forms of mental illness, once explained by demon possession, have been successfully naturalized. As you might expect, attempts to naturalize religious and moral behaviors have met with serious opposition. Mircea Eliade, the famous scholar of religion, persisted in claiming that religious behavior could not be naturalized because all forms of religion derive from encounters with the *sacred*, and the sacred was not open to naturalistic methods of inquiry.[2] Naturalists, of course, will disagree and press forward with attempts to naturalize all forms of religious experience and expression. We may say that an attempt to naturalize religion will be successful if it can give a plausible general account of the structure, the functions, and the origins of religious traditions.[3]

The place to begin is with a definition of wisdom: wisdom is the wherewithal to live in harmony with reality. Individuals and cultures may differ in their apprehensions of what is real, and they may disagree about how to live in harmony with it, but nowhere do we find traditions dedicated to living unwisely, that is, against the grain of the ultimately real. This definition of wisdom gives us a clue to understanding the nature of religion. Religious traditions are narrative traditions, each one with a distinctive story, a myth, at its core. A religious myth is the principal means by which the members of a culture come to share a common wisdom, a common understanding about how things are in the real world (cosmology), and about which things matter for human fulfillment (morality).

The distinctive feature of religious myths is that they manage to fuse cosmological ideas together with moral values to form an integrated story, wherein the cosmos is presented as a moral order and moral values acquire the status of facts. This integration of facts and values is enabled by the power of a root metaphor. Here's an illustration drawn from the Abrahamic traditions. The root metaphor of the Judeo-Christian-Muslim myth is the idea of God-as-person. God is pictured as the creator of the universe, the ultimate source of all that exists. God is also the author of moral law, such that God's will determines what is good and evil. The same agency, God, is therefore the ultimate *cosmological explanation* for every event that happens in the world, and the ultimate *moral justification* (or condemnation) for every action performed in the world. When members of a culture share a vision of how things ultimately are and which things ultimately matter, then they will have a common orientation in nature and history, an orientation that tells them where they came from, what their true nature is, and how they should live. And equipped with this wisdom they will be more likely to assess problematic situations in a common way, and respond to them with cooperative and predictable behavior.

It is important, therefore, that each mythic tradition develops strategies designed to assure that the ideas, attitudes, and values embodied by the story will find their way into the brains of all members of the social group, there to engage motivational systems and to influence behaviors in appropriate ways. Here we begin to see the distinctive *structure* of religious traditions: at their core is a story, a set of ideas and attitudes that integrate facts and values. And surrounding this central myth is a set of strategies designed to keep the tradition viable. These "myth supporting strategies" will include the following:

> *Intellectual strategies*, designed to maintain the intellectual plausibility and coherence of the central story by clarifying, interpreting and defending it.
>
> *Aesthetic strategies*, designed to engage emotional systems and memory systems with symbolic imagery, thereby to bias these systems toward behaviors that are consonant with the myth.
>
> *Ritual strategies*, designed to revitalize individual commitments to the myth by engaging in periodic social reenactment.
>
> *Experiential strategies*, designed to revitalize the myth by encouraging and enabling extraordinary experiences that function as personal validations of the myth.
>
> *Institutional strategies*, designed to manage the orderly social transmission of the myth, and to resolve conflicts that arise within the group.

The general *function* of religious traditions is to educate the emotions of individuals so that they will think, feel, and act in ways that are conducive to their personal and collective well-being. This general function may be seen in the way the supporting strategies bear upon aspects of human nature, and in doing so they engage individuals in the meanings of the myth. The strategies work together to bias the various neural systems that are responsible for mediating behavior. In particular, the supporting strategies are designed to engage the so-called social emotions in ways that enhance social cooperation.

Millions of years of evolution have equipped our species with a range of specific emotional systems that were selected for their powers to produce adaptive behaviors. Together, these systems may be seen to constitute a primitive system of morality. Emotional traits operate according to inherent rules—an "if-then" logic—such that if an individual is presented with a stimulus (say, an act of generosity by a conspecific), then he or she will be likely to experience gratitude, and will respond accordingly. The emotional toolkit of humans is much debated, but there is something approaching a consensus that it includes sympathy, resentment, gratitude, affection, guilt, disgust, anger, jealousy, and various shades of fear (e.g., awe, respect, humility).

These are the systems exploited by the ministrations of a religious tradition. In the primitive circumstances of the deep evolutionary past—when humans lived in small hunting-gathering groups—this emotional toolkit equipped our distant ancestors with an intuitive moral system. Social interactions were efficiently regulated by emotional gut reactions, not by an articulate moral code. The image of a social mobile aptly describes the sociality of these primitive ancestors—individuals bobbing and twirling in genetically scripted patterns as they acted out their gut feelings in response to the behavior of others, resulting in a relatively stable and predictable social order. The power of religious traditions to redirect and regulate the social mobile rests on their ability to manipulate the emotional toolkit by symbolic means. Consider, for example, how the image of an innocent man being tortured elicits a sympathetic response, or how images of an infant elicit affectionate responses, or how the bounty of creation elicits gratitude, or how images of heaven and hell inspire hope and fear.

When individuals become emotionally aroused in these ways they are more likely to act in conformity with the conventions of virtue promoted by the articulate moral code. For example, feelings of gratitude to God will dispose a person to obey God's will, as will the fear of hell or the promise of heaven. When the mythic strategies are working properly the result will be a pretty well regulated social order. And consider how these dynamics contribute to the achievement of a meaningful life as well. If I am motivated to serve God's will—the meaning of virtue—then I will be disposed toward a virtuous life. But if the ministrations of the tradition can manage to educate my desires, then I will be in such a state that nothing can make me happy but to act virtuously. And by this logic the twin telē of personality and sociality are advanced and the prospects for viability are increased. Religious traditions, as it turns out, serve biological functions.

The *origins* of religious traditions take us back to the great leap forward of about fifty thousand years ago. By that time, our ancestors certainly had language at their disposal, and it is very likely that they had developed articulate cosmologies to explain natural phenomena. These primitive cosmologies probably featured spirits and divine agents whose powers might have accounted for various mysteries, such as death, dreams, fertility, and the weather. But moral authority would not have been attributed to these agencies, for the very simple reason that primitive social units already had all the moral rules they needed, right where the genes had put them: in the emotional systems. As social units enlarged, however, there was a need for more complex rules for social regulation. The intuitive morality of untutored emotional systems was not up to the task. When social chaos loomed it fell to social dominants to declare law and order in the form of strange new articulate rules, and then to enforce them with threats of violence. When pressed with demands for justifying what must have seemed like arbitrary and counterintuitive rules, it would have been natural for the rule makers to attribute moral authority to the gods, who were already understood to wield power over natural forces. This attribution marked the origin of religion, for here was the first attempt to integrate cosmology and morality under the persuasive power of a root metaphor. The gods now had the dual role of explaining natural phenomena and justifying moral values. And once there was a basic story in place, the harmony and stability of an enlarged social order came to depend upon revitalizing the myth (read: educating the emotions) by deploying intellectual, aesthetic, ritual, experiential, and institutional strategies.

Hostility directed at those who attempt to naturalize religion has been motivated in part by the fear that religious truths might be "explained away" by the spirit of reductionism in the same manner, perhaps, that Santa Claus and the Easter Bunny are explained away. And this would be a great shame, it is felt, because religious traditions provide the sources of existential meaning for the vast majority of humankind. To naturalize religion, then, is to neutralize the meaning of life. Think of Isaiah's poor neighbors: What becomes of their piety once they pick up on Isaiah's insight that their wooden god is nothing but a sham? In addition to being morally culpable, it might appear that naturalists have an intellectual problem as well. That is, if naturalists truly believe that the real point of religious traditions is to advance biological functions, then isn't it ultimately maladaptive to debunk them with naturalistic explanations? And if so, then naturalizing religion would be inconsistent. When faced with these intellectual and moral indictments, naturalists typically take refuge in the very principle that sustains religious traditions themselves: it is always wise to live in harmony with reality. If naturalists have good reasons to believe that supernaturalist accounts of reality and value are unwise, then there can be no intellectual or moral wrongdoing in attempting to bring them down to earth. Religious naturalists might carry this line of reasoning one step farther to say that religious naturalism represents a genuinely religious orientation that is more adaptive than its alternatives.

The Heart of Naturalism

Historians of religion have warned us that all accounts of Hinduism are idiosyncratic, the reason being that "Hinduism" is a category invented by Western scholars for the sake of defining into existence a distinctive religious tradition. The truth of the matter, however, is that Hinduism is too pluriform to be captured by conventional categories. We are in much the same position with respect to naturalism. It is true that naturalists are united by a general metaphysical doctrine, and it is true that this predisposes naturalists toward certain epistemological and ethical views rather than others, but it is too much to ask for a non-idiosyncratic account of naturalism.

Metaphysics

Naturalism is a very general metaphysical doctrine. It simply declares that whatever is natural is real and whatever is real is natural. That is, reality does not break out into two realms, the natural and the super-natural. Naturalism rejects the notion that anything at all transcends nature, except nature itself. As a general orientation, naturalism is open to various specific interpretations. There persists a widespread assumption that naturalism is committed to a materialist metaphys-ics—the view that only matter is real—but this is simply false. Many naturalists are materialists, to be sure, but naturalism is logically compatible with the idealist view that nature is essentially mental, and also with metaphysical dualism, which says that nature consists of two distinct yet equally real substances: matter and mind. Hegel, for example, was a naturalist of the idealist sort, while Aristotle was a naturalist with dualist leanings.

Two of the most frequent objections naturalists must contend with are expressed in the following questions:

> How do you *know* there is nothing that transcends nature?
> How can naturalism possibly give an explanation for the
>   existence of nature itself?

The assumption behind the first question is that if naturalism cannot demonstrate the incoherence of supernaturalism, then naturalism must be false and, by default, supernaturalism must be true. To the first question naturalists will have two responses. The first response simply concedes that naturalism cannot demonstrate that nothing transcends nature. To be consistent, a naturalistic demonstration would have to be limited to evidence drawn from nature. But the task of providing natural evidence for the absence of something supernatural would surely be a fool's errand. So naturalists must plainly admit that they do not, and cannot, know that supernaturalism is false. A more substantive response to the first question, however, would be to challenge the presumption behind it. There is quite simply nothing in the naturalist's failure to make good on the first question that would entail either the falsehood of naturalism or the truth of supernaturalism. As for the default argument, the naturalist might turn it to an advantage, for while it may be true enough that "absence of evidence is not evidence of absence," it is also true that absence of evidence is absence of any sufficient or respectable reason to believe in something.

The second question is a variation on the problem of why something (i.e., nature) exists rather than nothing at all. Both forms of the question make the assumption that there *must be* an intelligible answer, and if naturalism cannot provide it then supernaturalism (which presumably can) must be true. Naturalists typically respond to this question by insisting that not all questions deserve to be given answers, and this question is chief among them. An alternative response would be to admit the question and then simply concede that naturalism cannot answer it. Nature is not enough to explain nature. But naturalists would amend this response by adding that supernaturalism cannot answer it either. The supernaturalist answer to the question—that nature exists because God willed it—merely gives the illusion of an intelligible answer. How are we to make sense of the claim that God willed the existence of the natural order if we cannot—as all responsible theists concede—begin to comprehend God? To say that nature exists because God willed it is merely to explain the impenetrable in terms of the inscrutable, or to clear up one mystery by introducing another. But even if we were able to make sense of the theistic answer we would be in no better shape because the claim that God caused nature to exist invites us to ask what caused God to exist. In other words, the claim that God is the explanation for nature sets in motion an infinite regression of questions, for we can immediately ask what explains God, and what explains the explanation for God, and so on. If the theist insists that God is a cause without a cause, then it would appear that we're right back to explaining mysteries in terms of mysteries.

The debate between naturalism and supernaturalism often turns on the question of miracles. Miracles are putative events that can be given no naturalistic explanation, but can be given a supernatural one. Suppose we hear that a man has turned into a radish and after a week he returns to life as a human. Such an event, if it happened, would defy all attempts at a naturalistic explanation, yet the event might be explained by divine agency. The failure of naturalism to explain such putative events is taken to demonstrate that nature is not enough. The naturalist response to miracles has consistently been that they don't happen, which is to say either that the event in question never occurred, or that it did occur and can be given a naturalistic explanation, even though one hasn't yet been found. On this point naturalism has an impressive display of analogous evidence, for it can cite countless examples of mysteries and wonders that have been shifted from the column of miraculous events to the column of natural events.

It should be noted that not all supernaturalists or theists engage in talk about miracles. Some, in fact, would accept the argument that the concept of miracle undermines more important theological ideas, such as the doctrine of creation or the divine attributes. Consider this: theism claims that God created the universe together with the laws of nature. The creation took place in accordance with God's will, as a means to achieve God's purposes. But if God is omnipotent and omniscient, then it may be presumed that God's ordained laws of nature will be sufficient for the sake of advancing God's purposes. A miracle, however, is understood as an event that violates natural laws at the behest of divine agency, presumably to advance some divine purpose. But if this is the case, then we must conclude that the laws of nature, ordained by God, were *not* sufficient to execute God's purposes—a result that appears to compromise claims to divine omnipotence and/or omniscience. In addition, one might proffer the suggestion that anyone responsible for pulling off a miracle is open to the charge of violating God's willed laws of nature. But a violation of God's will amounts to an act of sin, and if God is perfectly good then God cannot sin. So the concept of miracle can be seen to entail a situation where God works at cross-purposes with Godself, and should therefore be rejected, on theological grounds, as an incoherent concept.

This little discussion of miracles brings us to a general point about naturalism: its commitment to reducing all explanations to natural causes. The list of naturalized phenomena includes diseases, birth defects, astral displays, mental illness, death, dreams, fertility, the weather, and so on. But the list of naturalized phenomena will continue to grow as inquiry proceeds. Many opponents of naturalism, however, will insist that there are some phenomena that cannot be naturalized, such as the origins of life, the splendors of conscious experience, the dynamics of spiritual transformation, the moral conscience, or the power of faith. Naturalism does not pretend that all interesting and important phenomena are now, or ever will be, fully intelligible in terms of natural causes. It does maintain, however, that our ability to understand real phenomena—objects, events, properties, relations—is contingent on our efforts to naturalize them. Briefly put: to know is to naturalize.

Naturalism advances a broad and simple metaphysical claim: that the order of nature is all there is to reality. If something is claimed to be supernatural or unnatural or non-natural, then the naturalist will ascend to the nearest promontory to challenge the claim vigorously. By contrast, science (qua science) undertakes no metaphysical commitments whatsoever. It does not declare that the natural order of things is uniquely real, even though in practice it confines its inquiry exclusively to natural phenomena. Many serious scientists happen to be philosophical naturalists, but certainly not all of them are. Some, in fact, are certified supernaturalists who might even profess that their motivation to pursue science is inspired by supernatural commitments. The relationship between science and naturalism is slightly asymmetrical, that is, whereas science (qua science) is indifferent to the metaphysical claims of naturalism, the naturalist is hardly indifferent to science. And the reason, of course, is that science has been an indispensable ally in the project of naturalizing everything in sight.

To naturalize, however, is not to scientize. On this point we need to be clear because confusion abounds. Naturalists are commonly accused of advocating a view known as *scientism*, a body of philosophical claims about the privileged authority of the natural sciences. Scientism holds that the natural sciences constitute a magisterium on truth, that science is the final arbiter on all claims about how things are. According to scientism, science is the only legitimate avenue to truth, and any claims to know what science cannot know are not to be taken seriously. Critics of scientism have been quick to point out that scientism is *not science*; it is a philosophical position that goes well beyond the limits of responsible science. More seriously, scientism appears to be self-defeating because its central claim (that science provides the only legitimate warrant for belief) cannot itself be vouchsafe by scientific inquiry. Scientism, as some critics might gleefully put it, is the sort of doctrine that gets blown away by its own petard. My own instincts, as a naturalist, are to put some distance between naturalism and science without sacrificing the claim that the principles and methods of science represent a uniquely privileged form of inquiry. The trick is to formulate a responsible version of scientism. We shall return to this topic in the next section on epistemology.

It should be clear enough by now that the general perspective of naturalism isn't very complicated: naturalism advances the broad and simple metaphysical doctrine that nature is all there is to reality. There are, of course, many detailed variations on this simple doctrine—diverse views on the nature of "nature"—and a general survey of naturalism would quickly reveal that it is far more diverse and complicated than I've been letting on.

Knowledge and Inquiry

Seeking wisdom is a universal human trait. A few pages ago, wisdom was defined as the wherewithal to live in harmony with reality, and it takes little reflection to see why the search for wisdom is so important. If you fail to live in accord with the constraints and provisions of reality, then you are likely to perish, but if you succeed, then you are likely to flourish. It seems obvious, then, that wisdom and inquiry go hand in hand: in order to acquire wisdom we must inquire about the nature and dynamics of reality. If you take the view that a transcendent God is the ultimate reality, then it would make sense for you to concentrate your energies on inquiry into the nature and will of God. Thus, for example, it is not surprising that the Abrahamic traditions place so much emphasis on the study of scripture. Such inquiry is a serious religious concern: it is salvific. If you are a naturalist, however, taking the view that the natural order is ultimately real, then you will do well to focus your inquiry on nature. We may say, then, that inquiry into nature is close to the heart of naturalism. And this means, of course, that a commitment to scientific inquiry (the study of nature) is a central concern. If this is scientism, then so be it.

Before attempting to formulate a responsible version of scientism, I will insert a qualification about the inclusive nature of scientific inquiry. The word *science* literally means "knowledge," and I will assume that differences between the traditional sciences (physics, chemistry, biology, psychology, et al.) and other disciplines of human inquiry (art history, literary criticism, political science, religious studies, et al.) are differences of degree, not differences of kind. Paintings, poems, voting blocs, and religious traditions are natural phenomena as surely as molecules and thunderstorms are, and the study of natural phenomena is what we call science. Art historians, literary critics, and scholars of religion propose beliefs about natural phenomena, justifying these with evidence and arguments. The natural sciences are far more precise, to be sure, and their findings are much more reliable, but this is only because they focus on phenomena that are far less complex, involving orders of magnitude fewer variables. Molecules, for example, are far simpler, algorithmically, than reflex systems or economic fluctuations. I will continue to use the word *science* in the conventional sense, but with the understanding that it is not a qualitatively distinct mode of inquiry.

The way to proceed toward a responsible form of scientism is to put the sciences where they belong: squarely within the broader context of human inquiry. A responsible scientism will admit that our popular understanding of the scientific enterprise has been too heavily influenced by efforts to make it appear more exclusive and unadulterated than it really is. Science itself is a natural phenomenon, a fallible human endeavor, vulnerable to the full range of bungling and distortion that threatens human projects everywhere. Science does not—nor does a responsible scientism claim it does—deliver absolute truths about how things are in the order of nature. Scientists inquire just like the rest of us: they noodle around until they feel ready to propose beliefs about the world. The essential difference is that the hard sciences are more rigorously disciplined by techniques for minimizing extraneous and subjective factors. Human inquiry—science included—is primarily guesswork, but the sciences are distinguished by the reliability of their strategies for ruling out bad guesses, and for ascertaining the probabilities that the surviving guesses are in fact true beliefs about nature.

Beliefs cannot be more or less true: if something is the case, then it just is the case. Period. But matters are never quite this simple, which leaves us in a position of choosing among proposals for belief that have more or less justification in their favor. Truth, then, is hardly the question—what really matters in human inquiry is ferreting out well-justified proposals for belief. And this means evidence. Naturalists are evidentialists, which means they believe it is wise to apportion our beliefs to the abundance of available evidence—as the amount of evidence increases or decreases so does the strength of belief. In fact, we might even say that naturalists have something akin to reverence for evidence, not unlike the sort of reverence that Abrahamics feel in relation to their scriptures. Perhaps a parallel between "Thus saith the Lord" and "Thus indicates the evidence" is not out of place. Abrahamics revere scripture because they believe it is God's word, which means, in effect, that it imparts true beliefs. Naturalists have a similar reverence for evidence because it is a reliable guide to true beliefs. Consider two proposals, A and B. If one of these proposals, let's say A, has more evidence in its favor, then which of the two proposals is more likely to be true? Proposal A, of course. And this is why naturalists are committed to apportioning their beliefs to the abundance of available evidence: to do otherwise is palpably foolish.

Because inquiry and evidence are so close to the heart of naturalism, I will carry the discussion just a bit farther by offering a simple model for thinking about the structure of human inquiry. We might call this "a proposal for beliefs about proposals for belief." I find this model a helpful complement to the evidentialism that all naturalists share. The model amounts to a rank ordering of classes of belief in terms of their evidential justification. So here goes . . .

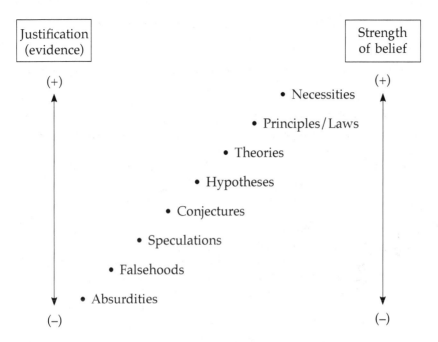

Figure 4.1.

Now the point will be to comment briefly on each of these categories of belief proposals, beginning with the least justified.

Absurdities have an absolute negative justification for belief. This is the class of logical impossibilities, such as, "it is Monday and it is not Monday." It is impossible to supply justification for believing absurdities because they are impossible to comprehend. If you encounter someone claiming to believe an absurdity there's nothing to do but administer a dope slap and call 911.

Falsehoods are logically possible proposals for belief having decisive (but not absolute) negative justification. Whereas absurdities are contradicted by themselves, falsehoods are contradicted by other propositions. If we have good reason (evidence) for believing proposal X, and if X contradicts Y, then Y has negative justification in proportion to the positive justification for X. In such cases we would say that Y has been falsified by X.

Speculations are logically possible proposals for belief, lacking any decisive justification or falsification. But beyond this, we cannot quite imagine what it would take to move us in one way or the other on the belief issue. Speculations have the appearance of being consistent with all justified proposals, but not being justified by any of them. We are speculating when we can imagine *that* something is the case, but we cannot imagine *how* it could be the case. It might be true and it might not, but there's no conceivable way to tell. With speculative proposals we have difficulty seeing how it might be possible to isolate relevant variables, or we find it impossible to formulate the proposal in a way that would suggest relevant evidence. In some cases speculative proposals involve more complexity than we are equipped to manage. Some would argue that the domain of metaphysics is a domain of speculation, where thought floats freely in the land of imagination, guesswork, and idle fancies. Speculative proposals may themselves be idle (because we are unable to assess them), but the *activity* of speculation is an immensely constructive part of all human inquiry—many of our most important beliefs started out as idle speculations. Because we cannot imagine what would justify or falsify speculative proposals we must say that while they are possible they are not plausible, which is to assign to them a very low probability of being true.

Conjectures are distinguished from speculations by this factor: we can imagine *that* a conjecture might be the case (as with speculations), but we can also imagine *how* it might be the case. That is, we can see what sort of evidence would count toward justification, even though we cannot imagine how to get it. Conjectures have weak justification, perhaps in the form of indirect or circumstantial evidence, or perhaps because they are analogous to other proposals. With conjectures we have a strong sense of relevant evidence and critical variables, so we know what to be on the lookout for, but we cannot see the practical means for bringing the relevant factors into play. In brief, conjectures are possible, coherent, and somewhat plausible, but because of mostly practical reasons they remain completely untestable. And for these reasons conjectures are to be regarded as improbable.

Hypotheses are literally (from the Greek) "proposed for belief." Absurdities are impossible to believe, falsehoods are not to be believed, speculations are hard to believe, and conjectures are barely believable. But hypotheses are well worth serious consideration for belief, for they are logically possible, eminently plausible and (until further notice) probable enough to warrant some benefit of doubt. We can see *that* they might be true, we can see *how* they might be true, and we are given a reasonably good chance of getting decisive evidence on the matter. We can predict, with a fair amount of certainty, what will happen in experimental settings if a hypothesis is true.

Theories are proposals for belief about how things are in the world at a high level of generality. A general formulation becomes established as a theory when it provides a compact and reliable explanation for a range of particular facts. Theories become progressively well justified as they continue to predict phenomena and as they continue to generate new speculations, conjectures, and hypotheses. Theories are logically possible, coherent, highly plausible, testable, and (most importantly) already tried and tested with positive results, which earns them a high probability of being true accounts of how things are. Whereas hypotheses warrant a suspension of doubt, theories warrant a presumption of truth.

Principles and Laws are the most general and most securely established descriptions of how things are in the natural order. While principles and laws—such as the principle of evolution or the laws of thermodynamics—are not absolutely true, their probability of truth is sufficiently high to place them beyond dispute. Given the rest of our beliefs, it is difficult to imagine how established principles and laws could not be true, which accounts for the fact that they are almost never debated in the course of inquiry.

Necessities have absolute positive justification for belief. It is logically impossible for them to be false. For example, "this bachelor is not married" is necessarily true. To believe a necessity it is sufficient merely to understand it.

We cannot leave this discussion without commenting briefly on the naturalist's dismissal of supernaturalist claims to revealed knowledge. Naturalist responses to these claims are keyed to the nature of the claims. Some theologians, for example, claim that knowledge about certain supernatural beings and events is evident in the phenomena of nature and history to all those who remain open to it. This is not unlike the claim that beauty is inherent in a painting or a poem to those who possess normal sensibilities. Naturalists typically reject this "natural" form of revelation as an exercise in zealous overinterpretation, akin to anthropomorphizing plant behavior. Special revelation, however, is a different matter. Here the assertion is that knowledge of supernatural realities is imparted to individuals by means that transcend all normal capacities for reason and sense. Naturalists have no interest in denying the intensity or the importance of these extraordinary experiences, but they will challenge their veracity on the suspicion that the dynamics of such deliverances tell us far more about the experiencing subjects than about the objects experienced. Naturalists therefore tend to regard reports of special revelation as delusional. Despite the impressive powers of the human brain for discernment and analysis, it is notorious for making occasional blunders, such as beholding things that aren't there or blocking out things that are. The dismissal of revelation as delusion sounds somewhat less harsh when the naturalist concedes that no one enjoys a delusion-free existence. We all possess brains that edit, redact, expunge, or enhance just about everything that comes along, and we all have our moments for getting things wrong. If the charge of delusion seems harsh it is only because the subject matter of the prophet's experience is so immensely consequential. Naturalists reserve their intentionally harsh criticisms for those who make claims to special revelation as a strategy for exempting knowledge claims from public scrutiny. Such claims are open to indictments of intellectual dishonesty, for they assert authority without accountability or justification.

Human Nature and Values

The metaphysical doctrine unifying all naturalists is, once again, that whatever is natural is real and whatever is real is natural. If moral behavior is real it is natural, and if it is natural it can in principle be explained by natural causes. All naturalists, therefore, take an interest in naturalizing the domain of ethics, just as they aspire to naturalize religious phenomena. Parts of the previous chapter addressed this issue, where it was argued that values (telē) originate as emergent properties inherent in all living systems, and that the function of telē-bearing traits is to promote viability. Certainly not all naturalists take this approach, however. Those naturalists who follow the strong reductionist thesis will deny that telē are real properties of nature, and will therefore conclude that moral values are illusory. By contrast, naturalists who accept the reality of telē (as I do) will identify themselves as moral realists, insisting that there are at least some values—inherent in at least some parts of nature—waiting to be discovered by inquiry.

Here another divide opens up between those naturalists who inquire after values inherent in the fabric of the cosmos, and those whose inquiry is confined to the adaptive traits of living organisms. But this is merely the beginning of diversity among ethical naturalists. Additional questions expose divisions between anthropocentrists, biocentrists, ecocentrists, deep ecologists, utilitarians, and so on. This is not the place, however, to survey the diversity among ethical naturalists. A far more important matter, for our purposes, is to address the principal objection to naturalizing morality.

In 1903 G. E. Moore proposed the "open question argument," which many observers take to be a defeater for naturalistic ethical theory.[4] Here's the way it works. One might very well agree that if something is good, then what *makes* it good is that it has certain inherent natural properties. For example, eyesight may be considered good because it is an adaptive trait—its adaptivity *makes* it good. Now, a person may agree with these statements and still not be satisfied with the account. Why? Because the question of what is good is left open. That is, we are still justified in asking, "Yes, I agree that eyesight is *adaptive*, but is it *good*?" The naturalist may respond by saying, "Of course it's good, *because* it's adaptive." At this point the objector, sensing triumph, will reply, "But this is merely to *equate* adaptivity with goodness—that *whatever* happens to be adaptive is good. And that cannot be the case, for we can easily imagine all sorts of adaptive traits (a disposition for rape?) that we would not judge to be good." The objector's point here is that the adaptivity of some trait or another leaves open the question of its goodness.

Moore's open question argument brings to light an important aspect of human nature: human beings are capable of doubting and disparaging the telē endowed on us by natural selection. That is, we have the cognitive wherewithal to reject inherent goals that nature has equipped us to desire in favor of desiring opposing goals of our own invention. To say it again: we have it in our power to behold ideals of goodness and to pursue goals that go against our nature. And this seems to imply that "the good" we apprehend is not a natural property, which further suggests that the moral life cannot be naturalized. The philosophical literature generated by Moore's critique of naturalism is vast, and it would take us too far afield to undertake a review here. What I will offer instead are two reasons why I think the open question argument does not decisively defeat naturalism.

To begin, it is not irrelevant that our ability to challenge the goodness of our inherent telē—what nature equips us to desire—is itself a function of an adaptive organ (the brain). Indeed, one of the principal functions of the brain is to sort through the conflicting impulses arising from a plurality of motivational systems and to resolve the conflict. At any given point in the life of a human being (or a chimp, for that matter) it is nearly inevitable that some inherent goods are casting other inherent goods into doubt. So there is nothing at all exceptional or unnatural about our embodying goals that challenge the goodness of our inherent goals.

What is most interesting about Moore's argument is that he presents us with the prospect of apprehending values that are not themselves "natural" in the sense of being inherent properties of biological traits. It is this feature—the potential for non-natural values to render judgments on natural ones—that creates an open question. In other words, there appears to be something we might call the "moral imagination," or "moral reason," that operates as a source of irreducible non-natural values and opens the question on all claims about the goodness of inherent values.

What are we to make of this supposed faculty of moral imagination? Well, it might be said that the moral imagination is a pretty good name for the emergent property of self-assessment that was described in connection with the great leap forward, when novel social relationships called into play new dynamics of self-consciousness in the form of self-monitoring and group identity. In the context of the great leap forward, we argued, doubting the goodness of our gut reactions (inherent telē) and coming up with concepts involving counterintuitive goals was part of the new social contract. That's what the introduction of an articulate moral system was all about. In other words, given the emergent events of the great leap forward, the "open question" problem is precisely what we should expect to find. In the great leap forward the question of human existence and meaning was irreversibly opened. But there are no good reasons to see these developments as inexplicable in terms of natural causes.

The other reason for disregarding Moore's critique has to do with the extraordinary and unique character of viability as a moral value. Early in the previous chapter I claimed that we are justified in asserting that viability qualifies as the one and only objective moral standard. The claim was that if anything is good, then life is good. Now it may be asked whether Moore's argument opens the question on the goodness of life. Can we see the question, "Yes, it's adaptive, but is it good?" on equal footing with "Yes, it's living, but is it good?"? Perhaps, but I cannot see it. The first challenges a way of living, but the second challenges life itself. A petulant naturalist might try to reverse the issue and open questions for non-naturalists: "You say this is *good*, but is it *adaptive*?"[5]

Open questions or not, naturalists tend to move quickly through semantic gymnastics and get on with the business of conducting moral inquiry as a form of applied experimental science. For naturalists, morality makes no sense apart from empirical inquiry into human nature. When one considers the first rule of moral reasoning—"ought implies can"—it becomes impossible to disagree. Before pronouncing on what humans *ought* or *ought not* to do, we need to know what they *can* and *cannot* do—that is, reliable knowledge about human possibilities, limitations, and dispositions is prerequisite to all rational moral discourse.

Naturalists, then, begin moral inquiry with the sciences of human nature. Steven Pinker identifies the central disciplines as cognitive science, neuroscience, behavioral genetics, and evolutionary psychology.[6] A loose amalgam of these disciplines travels under the heading, "evolutionary moral psychology." The point of the sciences of human nature is to assemble a sort of user's manual—statistical and time-sensitive, of course—for working with human beings, that is, a body of knowledge telling us how evolution has equipped our species with behavioral mechanisms for negotiating a livelihood in physical and social environments. To understand these endowments is to understand the general human strategies for achieving viability. To understand these endowments is also to possess what is arguably the most important of all resources for the moral life: a set of standards for ruling out bad guesses about moral truths.

Let me repeat what was said a few pages ago about the conduct of science. Scientists inquire just like everyone else: they noodle around until they feel ready to propose beliefs about the world, and then they apply strategies for ruling out the bad guesses. When they have plausible guesses (hypotheses), they run experiments to see what happens. Naturalists are inclined to approach ethics on the same model of inquiry. They don't much care how ideas about moral values get generated by the moral imagination. Some are perhaps suggested by what we know of human nature, and others just naturally bubble up from noodling about a better world. But when the ideas enter into public discourse the naturalist will apply the sciences of human nature for the sake of eliminating the really bad proposals (e.g., "Thou shalt photosynthesize!" or "Thou shalt never become angry or resentful!"). As speculations and conjectures about moral truths reach the level of plausible hypotheses, naturalists are inclined to put them to the test in personal and social experiments. And then wait. Naturalists seek moral truths in the same manner as they seek truths about nature, for the simple reason that moral truths *are* truths about nature. This procedure avoids all the bother about open questions and naturalistic fallacies, while preserving the naturalist's fundamental insight that nature is enough.

Taking Nature to Heart

Religion and Spirituality

It is commonly assumed that theists of the supernaturalist variety are by definition religious, and that naturalists of any variety are by definition nonreligious. Both of these assumptions are hugely mistaken. In fact, many self-declared theists neither engage in religious practices, nor express what might be called religious or spiritual sensibilities. And, meanwhile, many naturalists do.

Before we can make any progress in a discussion of religious naturalism it will be necessary to clarify our terms. Many individuals—theists and non-theists alike—will balk at the word *religious* because they take it to imply conformity with institutionalized teachings and practices. And many naturalists balk at the word *spiritual* because they take it to imply belief in some supernatural being or metaphysical substance. I wish to be clear about rejecting both of these usages in favor of a single definition that treats "religious" and "spiritual" as equivalent terms. I regard a religious or spiritual person to be *one who takes ultimate concerns to heart*. The important difference between religious (spiritual) persons and nonreligious (nonspiritual) persons is a matter of attitudes. Attitudes are valenced beliefs, that is, beliefs that are infused with appraisals of value and existential meaning, beliefs that have non-trivial consequences for the way a person relates to something or someone. The difference between a religious theist and a nominal theist is that the former takes God to heart. Likewise, a religious naturalist differs from a nonreligious naturalist by virtue of his or her suite of attitudes: the religious naturalist takes nature to heart.

Nature means more to a religious naturalist than to a "plain old" naturalist. But from this it must not be inferred that religious naturalists are necessarily at odds with plain old naturalists concerning the reality of any entities, events, properties, or relations in the world. Nature means more to religious naturalists because they take nature to heart in ways that differently shape their thinking about nature, how they feel about it, and of course what they are disposed to say about it. It might be said that religious naturalists make different attributions concerning nature without making different claims.

The concept of taking something to heart warrants further reflection. One wants to know, for example, what sorts of things might be taken to heart, and what taking them to heart really means. We often speak of taking proposals, warnings, advice, or lessons to heart. Items taken to heart have significant potential for changing something fundamental in a person's life. Taking something to heart suggests that the thing is being treated as vitally important, that something is being put into play as a central element. If I take something to heart I invite it to have some measure of transformative power, I take active ownership of it, or I defer to it at a deeply personal level. Items taken to heart become part of what one apprehends as wisdom, that is, part of one's internal makeup, an essential feature in one's algorithms for living. I want to suggest that taking something to heart bears heavily on fundamental matters of purpose and meaning. It has everything to do with the process of personal growth, with altering the hierarchy of an individual's goals and values. If I were to say that I have taken the Koran to heart you might infer that the teachings of the Koran now shape how I think, feel, and act. I now take Allah's will as my own, and I have a newly clarified sense of who I am, where I came from, and where I am going. Taking the Koran to heart alters the fabric of my self-understanding, it shifts my teleological center of gravity, I operate differently in my efforts to live in harmony with reality.

It is difficult to see how a naturalist's taking nature to heart differs in any important sense from a theist's taking God to heart. Consider the ways both parties speak. Religious naturalists typically refer to nature as "sacred," in the sense of being inviolate and worthy of deep reverence. Religious naturalists are also likely to regard nature as creative and dynamic, not unlike traditional theistic talk about God. The religious naturalist will speak of nature as being, paradoxically, both intelligible and deeply mysterious, in parallel with theistic language about the revealed and hidden natures of God. For religious naturalists nature is ultimately real, the supreme giver of life, the source and destiny of all that is. Nature is that "in which we live and move and have our being," to borrow a phrase that St. Paul borrowed from the Stoics. Nature is self-sufficient, sovereign, omnipotent. Theistic language about the judgment and grace of God is roughly paralleled by the religious naturalist's assertion that nature constrains and enables. Theists claim that God transcends nature, while religious naturalists—especially the emergentists among them—will say that nature transcends nature itself.

There is no good reason to believe that taking nature to heart leaves a person with any fewer spiritual benefits than taking to heart the teachings of supernaturalist traditions. The self-understanding of religious naturalists may be radically transformed by taking the narrative of cosmic evolution to heart; their goal hierarchies may come to resonate with deep patterns in natural phenomena; they may experience a newfound sense of compassion and solidarity with other creatures; they may gain an enhanced appreciation for the complexity and beauty of creation; they may be moved by emotional responses to undertake morally constructive and spiritually satisfying projects; and they may come to know the serenity of assurance that they are living in harmony with reality. Isn't this enough? Donald Crosby believes it is:

This nature to which we intimately belong—a nature that sustains, renews, and inspires us in countless ways—can command our wholehearted religious commitment. We have no need of God, gods, animating spirits, or other sorts of putative religious objects, nor do we need to pine for another life in another realm beyond the wondrous home we find already in our natural world. Nature itself, when we rightly conceive of it and comprehend our role within it, can provide ample context and support for finding purpose, value and meaning in our lives.[7]

Unity and Diversity

The question is no longer whether naturalists can be genuinely religious. Of course they can be, in every meaningful sense. A more complicated question is whether there is potential for religious naturalism to develop into a recognizable religious tradition. This chapter opened with a brief discussion of the nature of religious traditions. To repeat, every religious tradition centers on a myth, a narrative integration of cosmological and moral ideas. And these myths are supported by various strategies designed to clarify, defend, revitalize, and transmit the central mythic vision. The question at hand is whether religious naturalism answers to this description of religion. It is really a question about what, if anything, unifies religious naturalists.

Cosmology. To begin, it is fairly evident that religious naturalists share a common cosmological vision. In fact, it is likely that there exists a greater consensus among religious naturalists about cosmology than might be found in virtually any other tradition on the planet. And the reason is not difficult to see. Ancient religious traditions are losing their sense of a shared worldview because of the serious tensions between their original cosmological ideas and the ideas of contemporary science. Consider the biblical myth, for example. The cosmology of the Bible offers a six-thousand-year-old three-storied universe, a six-day creation, dozens of stupendous miracles, and a grunge theory of matter. There is no question that this cosmological vision has been falsified by centuries' worth of responsible scientific inquiry. Of course, many Christians fully accept the cosmology of contemporary science, but the fact remains that many others do not. And many more are lost somewhere between the first century and the twenty-first century. The idea that Christians share a common story about how things are in the world is simply not true, and most other religious traditions are faced with the same problem.

Religious naturalists, however, are not troubled by a glaring discrepancy between their "received" cosmology and contemporary science because their received cosmology precisely *is* the cosmology of contemporary science. It is the narrative of cosmic evolution, the grand epic of emergent cosmogenesis from the Big Bang to the present day. So if sharing fundamental ideas—e.g., the nature of the cosmos, how the world works, the nature of humankind, the conditions of human existence—is important for the integrity of a religious tradition, then we would have to agree that religious naturalism is holding a pretty impressive hand.

Piety. In addition to sharing a common narrative of cosmogenesis, we might venture to say that religious naturalists are united by a common pattern of piety. Perhaps it is a mistake to introduce such a loaded term, but if we take care to reload it properly we may find it useful. "Piety" is normally used synonymously with "faith," a term that has been sadly corrupted over the centuries to connote "belief despite the evidence." Here I will use the term *piety* to mean a suite of attitudes and dispositions that arise when someone takes certain values, ideas, and principles to heart. When a Jew takes the law to heart, then he or she enters an integrative state, or acquires a persistent trait, characterized by fidelity, devotion, commitment, or submission to the law. Pious Jews, Muslims, Christians, et al., are the ones who have taken their stories to heart.

Brian Swimme is curious about how plain old naturalists become pious naturalists:

> The question that intrigues me now is this: what is it that happens that leads a person to regard cosmogenesis as not just a scientific theory, or a string of empirical facts, but as a way of life: as a religious attitude that enables a fresh, and creative, and cosmological orientation within the world?[8]

The answer to this question is that the process happens naturally. It may be complicated by more psychological variables than we can manage to identify precisely, but this does not alter the fact that many naturalists become genuinely pious. And when they do, they begin to sound like Joanna Macy:

> Come back with me into a story we all share, a story whose rhythm beats in us still. The story belongs to each of us and to all of us, like the beat of this drum, like the heartbeat of our living universe.

There is science now to construct the story of the journey we have made on this earth, the story that connects us with all beings. There is also great yearning and great need to own that story—to break out of our isolation as persons and as a species and recover through that story our larger identity. The challenge to do that now and burst out of the separate prison cells of our contriving, is perhaps the most wonderful aspect of our being alive today.

Right now on our planet we need to remember that story—to harvest and taste it. For we are in a hard time, a fearful time. And it is the knowledge of the bigger story that is going to carry us through. It can give us the courage, it can give us the strength, it can give us the hilarity to dance our people into a world of sanity. Let us remember it together.[9]

Some religious naturalists are brought to the story of cosmogenesis by their experiences of nature, and others are brought to experience nature by their acquaintance with the cosmic story, but the coupling of experience with cosmology is a distinctive feature in the piety of all religious naturalists. Acquaintance with the narrative of cosmogenesis opens individuals to deeper experiences of the natural world, which in turn drives them to seek a deeper understanding of the narrative. This coupling generates a suite of attitudes that we may call the piety of religious naturalism.

Religious naturalists bear an attitude of *reverence* toward the universe as a whole, and toward the earth in particular—and they are disposed to expressing their reverence by affirming that nature is both sacred and mysterious. Naturalists are keenly aware of the contingency of all life forms, and when this awareness is taken to heart it generates a sense of *gratitude* toward nature. Apprehension of the age and the magnitude of the universe, together with an apprehension of the astonishing complexity of natural systems leaves religious naturalists with a deep sense of *awe* and *humility*. All naturalists know that they are thoroughly natural beings, created by and embedded within both physical and social systems. And as these truths are taken to heart the pious naturalist acquires a sense of *connectedness* with the universe. Religious naturalists feel the comfort of being at home in the cosmos because they know from whence they came. The deep sense of relatedness experienced by religious naturalists also predisposes them to *tolerance, sympathy,* and *compassion* toward all other living things. In addition, religious naturalists are inspired with *hope* that scientific inquiry will continue to enrich our understanding and provide new resources for addressing challenges to viability.

Morality. Religious naturalists share a cosmology, and they are unified by a common pattern of piety. It now remains to ask whether there exists a common moral vision among religious naturalists. In the previous chapter I suggested that the telos of viability is inherent in the world, that is, scripted into the behavioral mechanisms of all living systems. All forms of life have been selected *for* carrying on. This way of putting things enables us to see that the narrative of emergent cosmogenesis integrates facts and values, cosmology and morality. And this integration, we saw, was the defining characteristic of a mythic tradition. But the moral vision inherent in the story of cosmic evolution is minimalist, to say the least. For humans it means merely that we will be driven to act out the gut reactions ordained by our various emotional systems—a moral "vision" that would restrict our species to a campsite existence. The social transformation associated with the great leap forward, however, introduced new dynamics of self-consciousness and group identity, together with the need to invent more complex articulate moral codes. Hence, religious traditions emerged to tell stories that integrated cosmological ideas with articulate moral imperatives.

It goes without saying that thousands of such traditions have presented themselves over the past fifty thousand years, among which religious naturalism represents a distinctive and very recent example. Naturalists who have taken nature to heart will experience a dramatic shift in self-identity, generating a radically new apprehension of what human beings are *for*. Reverence, gratitude, humility, connectedness, tolerance, and compassion will significantly alter the dynamics of self-consciousness and group identity. Just as new social relations called forth an emergent social order in the great leap forward, so does a new set of relations with the universe and other living creatures result in an emergent mentality. Gradually—or suddenly in some cases—the scope of one's affections expands beyond the self and the local group to include all humanity as well as all other species of life. One's understanding of viability is thus radically transformed when it is seen that achieving personal wholeness and social coherence is dependent on the integrity of the entire biosphere. Being *for* viability now begins to mean being *for* the integrity and sustainability of the earth's life support systems. Religious naturalists are thus united by a central myth that integrates an evolutionary cosmology with a biocentric morality. Herein lies the secret to a meaningful life for religious naturalists: they love nature, they explore and celebrate the mysteries of matter, and nothing makes them happier than pursuing goals that enable the viability of the biosphere.

Our question has been whether religious naturalism has the potential to develop into a robust religious tradition. It is clear that religious naturalists are united by a compelling myth as well as a distinctive pattern of piety. Its advocates find it to be an "ample context" for achieving a rich and meaningful life. So why is it that an intellectual/spiritual/moral vision having so much going for itself hasn't blossomed into a full-fledged religious tradition? Why don't we see religious naturalists assembling into congregations and establishing seminaries and drafting creeds, and all the rest of the trappings typical of flourishing religious traditions? If nature is enough, then why haven't we seen religious naturalist sanctuaries popping up all over the map in the way evangelical churches have been? The critics of religious naturalism claim to have the answer: the reason for religious naturalism's failure to make a mark on the religious hit parade is that nature, finally, is *not* enough.

Is Nature Enough?

John Haught, a prominent Roman Catholic theologian at Georgetown University, has been among the most thoughtful and passionate critics of naturalism. He has argued that naturalism lacks the resources necessary for satisfying our deepest intellectual and spiritual longings.

Intellectual Resources

Haught takes care in providing a clear and fair characterization of his target. He defines scientific naturalism (scientism) in the following seven points:

1. Outside nature, which includes humans and their cultural creations, there is nothing.

2. It follows from #1 that nature is self-originating.

3. Since there is nothing beyond nature, there can be no overarching purpose or transcendent goal that would give any lasting meaning to the universe.

4. There is no such thing as the "soul," and no reasonable prospect of conscious human survival beyond death.

5. The emergence of life and mind in evolution was accidental and unintended.

6. Every natural event is itself the product of other natural events. Since there is no divine cause, all causes must be purely natural causes, in principle accessible to scientific comprehension.

7. All the various features of living beings, including humans, can be explained ultimately in evolutionary, specifically Darwinian, terms.[10]

Haught makes it clear from the start that scientific naturalism is not itself supported by scientific inquiry. It may be true that many scientists will sign on to all seven points in the definition above, but they do so by virtue of their philosophical commitments, not their science. This said, Haught presents a series of arguments designed to demonstrate that naturalism is explanatorily insufficient and conceptually incoherent. His particular arguments contribute to a comprehensive default argument that asks readers to choose between the truth of naturalism and the truth of supernaturalism. In other words, if naturalism fails, then supernaturalism must, by default, be true. The comprehensive argument runs something like this:

1. There must be intelligible explanations for the existence of the natural order, and for all natural phenomena.[11]

2. Naturalism *cannot* give coherent and satisfying explanations for the existence of the natural order, or for certain distinctive natural phenomena.[12]

3. Supernaturalism *can* give coherent and satisfying explanations for the existence of the natural order, and for these distinctive natural phenomena.[13]

4. Naturalism cannot demonstrate that supernaturalism is false.[14]

5. Therefore, some form of supernaturalism is true.[15]

Most naturalists will find it difficult to take Haught's comprehensive argument seriously. The difficulties lie in the first and third premises. Many naturalists will accept the first premise, and indeed, they might even claim that a commitment to the first premise is ultimately what motivates scientific inquiry. But many naturalists will reject the first premise. For one thing, it might be the case that the natural order is eternal, in which case it would not need an explanation. This is precisely the strategy taken by many theists when asked for an explanation of God's existence. And for another thing, even if there *were* an explanation for the existence of the natural order, it may well be the case that it is beyond all human powers of comprehension. To suppose that humans are capable of understanding everything strikes many naturalists as naive and unwarranted presumption.

The first premise is therefore deeply problematic, but the most serious problems with the argument come from the third premise. The third premise can be no stronger than *specific explanations* make it, and if the specific explanations bring God into the picture, then one is justified in asking about the nature of God. But if the nature of God is ultimately incomprehensible (as Haught himself admits),[16] then it follows that supernaturalism is no better equipped to provide coherent and satisfying explanations of nature than naturalism is. You can't explain obscurities by reference to obscurities. Such logic, however, has never been sufficient to discourage the theological imagination.

Much of Haught's energy is given to supporting the second and third premises. There are certain phenomena in nature, he insists, that cannot be naturalized, which leaves open the door for more ultimate, supernaturalist, accounts. The claim is that what we *really* want to know about matter, life, and mind eludes the explanatory powers of science. Let's be clear: John Haught is no simpleminded creationist who opposes scientific explanations at every turn. He is, in fact, a strong advocate for the scientific enterprise, and he favors attempts to naturalize everything in sight, insofar as it is possible. Yet he is convinced that there are limits to naturalizing phenomena, and when we hit those limits we must turn to theology to get completely satisfying explanations. Nature is enough for explaining weather systems, earthquakes, and diseases, but there is something deeper about matter, life, and mind that naturalism cannot account for.

What is it, then, about matter, life, and mind—the natural order generally—that science cannot grasp? Haught's claim is that everywhere you look in the natural world there is undeniable evidence of an *anticipatory aspect* that science is powerless to make intelligible. The element of anticipation is most evident in the intentional quality of human experience, but it is also evident in the goal-directed behavior of all living organisms. Haught extends the concept of anticipation to include the cosmos as a whole. Nature itself is anticipatory, and science cannot explain this phenomenon:

Here again nature gives evidence of carrying a fundamentally anticipatory orientation that overflows the boundaries of the naturalist philosophy and calls out for an alternative worldview. The aspect of anticipation—by which I mean openness to new possibilities—that has always undergirded cosmic emergence comes to the surface most explicitly in the phenomena of subjectivity, sentience and striving. Hence it is not natural selection but something much more fundamental, namely, nature's anticipatory deportment, that provides the deepest subsoil of both life and suffering.[17]

Haught's "anticipatory aspect" boils down to a stylistic way of talking about teleology. If this interpretation is fair, then he is quite right to say that life and mind are irreducibly anticipatory. But there are two additional claims made by Haught that emergence-minded naturalists would challenge: one is that the cosmos itself is purposeful, and the other is that teleological phenomena cannot be naturalized. It is on these points that Haught's attitude toward naturalism gets a bit surly. On the first point—that the cosmos is anticipatory—Haught appears to be assuming the strong inherentist view that telē must be woven into the basic fabric of reality from the beginning. He, like Whitehead, regards the emergence of life from lifeless components or mind from mindless components to be logically impossible.[18] Instead, there must be some sort of metaphysical premonition, or anticipatory aspect, already present in nature.

In other words, Haught rejects the emergence view that radically new systemic properties of nature can arise spontaneously from modifications and amplifications of component relationships. If he accepted emergence theory he would have to acknowledge the plausibility of the naturalist's claim that purposeful behavior can emerge spontaneously within a purposeless universe. But this he is unwilling to do. Stranded, however, without a coherent critique of emergence theory, Haught resorts to the caddy instruments of rhetorical dismissal. Emergence theory, he inveighs, amounts to "magic," "superstition," "sorcery," "irrationality," "alchemy," "divination," "gratuitous leaps," "miraculous saltations," "unscientific reasoning," and (!) "necromancy."[19] Some argument!

In addition to the charge of explanatory insufficiency, Haught charges naturalism with conceptual incoherence. The argument here is inspired by his claim that human beings are so constituted that they cannot possibly resist trusting in the deliverances of their own minds:

"Your whole cognitional performance depends on a deeply personal confidence in your own intelligence and critical capacities."[20] What this means is that human beings have it in their nature to hold the truth in high regard. Seeking the truth, valuing the truth, and trusting our minds to apprehend it is part of our anticipatory nature. Even naturalists cannot resist this regard for the truth—it is the bedrock of scientific inquiry. With this truth-regarding principle in hand, Haught poses the following question: *Is the creed of naturalism consistent with the trust that you are now placing in the imperatives of your mind?*"[21] The answer, he says, is No.

Haught believes that naturalism cannot account for our inherent regard for truth. When trying to give an account of human knowledge the best naturalism can come up with is the principle that we are geared up to acquire *adaptive* beliefs, not *true* ones. Furthermore, naturalist accounts of human knowledge stress the vulnerability of our knowledge acquisition systems to error and deception. The gist of Haught's argument is that naturalism predisposes us to *doubt* the imperatives of our minds. But this is counterintuitive, since we cannot resist *not* doubting them. Thus, naturalism cannot give a coherent account of the essence of our cognitive lives. What's more, naturalists are inconsistent in the sense that they cannot practice what they preach: "So if adaptive evolution, or accidents of nature, or social conditioning . . . constitute the *ultimate* explanation of your own mental functioning, then why are you not suspicious right now that you may be deceiving me and yourself by claiming that naturalism is true?"[22]

Haught's arguments for the explanatory weakness and conceptual incoherence are designed to demonstrate that we need a theological vision in order to have a satisfying and reasonable account of natural phenomena: "I have made no secret of my belief that a fuller explanation of nature, one that can account for the element of anticipation in life, emergence, evolution and intelligence, requires, in addition to scientific study, the illumination of a theological worldview."[23] These arguments, however, do not succeed, and the reasons may be easily stated. For one thing, Haught appears to be under the misapprehension that science is wedded to a grunge theory of matter.[24] Consequently, he supposes that there can be no naturalistic way to account for the emergence of genuine novelty in the course of cosmic evolution, including novel dynamics in causal properties. But if models of emergence, of the sort proposed by Deacon and others, are taken seriously, then there is no reason to suppose that novelty is simply the outcropping of potentialities seeded into reality from the start. But Haught offers nothing substantial in the way of showing emergence theory to be implausible. All of which relieves us of the desperate search for supernatural principles of explanation, with all the obscurities and confusions pertaining thereto.

Regarding the charge of conceptual incoherence, the obvious naturalistic response would be the approach—previously mentioned—taken by Thomas Nagel.[25] Nagel's point was that humans have evolved with the rather special self-corrective ability to vacillate between states of commitment (trusting our minds) and states of self-doubt (not trusting our minds). It would hardly be worth the effort for a competent naturalist to draft a compelling argument showing that the reflective ability to occasionally doubt what we normally trust is far more adaptive than an irresistible urge to trust that what we apprehend is necessarily true. Normally we trust our cognitive deliverances, to be sure, but we are well served by periodic moments of self-doubt. Belief and doubt are equally adaptive. This is most certainly true.

Spiritual Resources

For John Haught, religion and naturalism are diametrically opposed. In fact, he takes pains to define matters in such a way that nature could not possibly be enough to satisfy our spiritual longings: "Religion, taken here in a very broad sense, is a *conscious appreciation of and response to the mystery that grounds, embraces and transcends both nature and ourselves.*"[26] Religion can get along just fine with science, but it cannot get along with naturalism for the simple reason that "religious naturalism" is an oxymoron, a logical monstrosity.[27] To religious ears, "nature is enough" sounds as dreary and suffocating as a prison sentence. To naturalists, meanwhile, it would appear that Haught's understanding of the religious quest—to get beyond nature—amounts to an utter delusion, for if there is one thing naturalism denies it is the pretentious ambition of human beings to transcend the natural order.

Haught is aware, of course, that there are more than a few individuals out there who self-identify as religious naturalists. What is to be said of them? Religious naturalists, he says, "hold that nature's overwhelming beauty, the excitement of human activity, the struggle to achieve ethical goodness, the prospect of loving and being loved, the exhilaration of scientific discovery—these are enough to fill a person's life. There is simply no good reason to look beyond nature for spiritual contentment."[28] Haught calls such individuals "sunny" naturalists, in contrast to "sober" naturalists who affirm that nature is devoid of meaning and cannot—as nothing can—possibly satisfy the deepest longings of our restless hearts. For sober naturalists, life is absurd because there is a fundamental incongruity between what humans want (more and more life) and what the universe offers (decay and final death). Steven Weinberg is, for Haught, the quintessential sober naturalist. Weinberg writes, "There are some among my scientific colleagues who say that the contemplation of nature gives them all the spiritual satisfaction that others have found in a belief in an interested God. Some of them may even feel that way. I do not."[29] Haught sees sober naturalists as hopelessly tragic, but they are at least honest about the implications of naturalism. By contrast, he sees the groundless optimism of religious naturalists as cowardly and deluded.[30]

We appear to be at an impasse, where religious naturalists and supernaturalists are left to hurl accusations of spiritual delusion back and forth. Each side has defined the religious life in terms that rule out the possibility of genuine piety for the other. Haught believes that all humans possess a deep spiritual longing for eternal life, and that naturalism can never satisfy this aspect of our nature. Naturalists, meanwhile, insist that belief in eternal life amounts to mere wish-fulfillment, and that mature persons should embrace a religious vision more harmonious with reality.

At the end of the day, it is clear that the most Haught can get from his investment is the weak conclusion that *nature is not enough for some people*. This may be something, but it's not enough.

The Promise of Religious Naturalism

Haught's arguments against the intellectual and spiritual virtues of religious naturalism fail to produce the results he intended. But we are still left with an unanswered question: If nature is enough, then why isn't religious naturalism more evident in public life? This is difficult to say. Why do so many great books and great movies fail to attract the public attention they deserve? No one knows.

At a distance, and on paper, there is much to attract and unify religious naturalists: a compelling cosmology, a robust piety, and a commanding moral vision. But when you get up close and personal there appear to be obstacles to the promise of religious naturalism. For one thing, there is the "God question." Some naturalists, such as Frank Lloyd Wright, seem perfectly happy to use the word: "I believe in God, only I spell it Nature." But others are fiercely opposed to the G-word, some because such a loaded term creates nothing but confusion and misunderstanding, and others because it carries unpleasant associations. Many religious naturalists are prone to anthropomorphize nature ("God's body"), but others find such images intolerable. The word *religious* is also offensive to some because it connotes super-naturalism, but others retain warm feelings toward the term. Some religious naturalists believe, as did Aristotle, that the cosmos is thoroughly imbued with telē, while others think purpose is an exclusive property of living systems. Some religious naturalists tend toward new age romanticism, while others insist on scientific rigor. Pantheists (who, by the way, have both a Web site and a creed)[31] have positioned themselves to lead a global movement of religious naturalists, but the results of their membership outreach have not been impressive. Serious religious naturalists are perhaps more likely to unleash their spiritual energies by attaching themselves to environmental activist groups. There is also the question about panentheists, those folks who see nature as part (but not all) of God's reality. Some naturalists regard this view as a simple variation on supernaturalism, but others aren't so sure. And on top of all this, religious naturalism is burdened with a cultural stigma. Its message is perceived to be hostile and negative toward the religious life. However sunny they might actually be, religious naturalists are still naturalists, which puts them squarely in the company of aggressive cranks and party-poopers such as Richard Dawkins and Sam Harris. Basically, then, the situation is this: religious naturalism may be compelling, coherent, and tidy in principle, but in fact it is ragged, unruly, and tainted with negativity. No one should expect religious naturalism to grow and galvanize into a recognizable movement or tradition anytime soon. There are too many obstacles and divisive factors in the way, and not nearly enough historical momentum to overturn them.

Having said all this, I fully expect the day to arrive when religious naturalism will prevail as the most universal and influential religious orientation on the planet. The source of my confidence in this prediction is the epic of cosmogenesis itself. Given a chance, this story is too compelling, too beautiful, too edifying, and too liberating to fail in captivating the imagination of a vast majority of humankind. And as long as I am in the prophetic mode I will go ahead and briefly sketch out two possible scenarios by which the global dominance of religious naturalism might come to pass. The first (more likely) scenario unfolds by a quick and dirty process, while the second (more palatable) process is slow and steady.

The global environmental crisis is now so widespread and so advanced that we might reasonably expect to see a collapse of natural and social systems on a global scale sometime within the next fifty years, resulting in a massive dieback of the human population and a descent into a dark age of decivilization. The global human population is presently at seven billion, and is projected to rise to nearly ten billion by the year 2050. We are already exceeding the earth's carrying capacity at present levels of population and consumption, with the result that every one of the earth's life-support systems—air, water, soil, climate, biodiversity—is in a state of serious decline. We are living way beyond sustainable levels of population and consumption, and our natural and social systems are stressed to the point of exhaustion and collapse. The prospects for reversing our behavior patterns in time to prevent a global holocaust are not in the least promising. It is probable, therefore, that we are destined for a global disaster of unprecedented and unimaginable proportions. Under the conditions of a global collapse of social systems human life will be pitched into chaos. In an earlier book I envisioned the holocaust in these terms:

> Supplies of vital resources diminish, and competition for them grows increasingly ugly and dangerous; important industries begin to falter and fold; unemployment skyrockets; homelessness increases; individuals become progressively more fearful, anxious, suspicious, uncooperative, devious and desperate; inflation soars; gangs coalesce; crime becomes rampant; raids on hoarders are commonplace; vigilante groups organize; public services decline; cities grow unmanageable and squalid; utilities become undependable; riots, looting, and fires ravage whole cities; schools close; nothing gets repaired; water and food become increasingly scarce and putrid; diseases spread; healthcare systems buckle; sickness and death at every hand; armed conflicts flare up in city streets; refugees, scavengers, and shanty towns everywhere; border incidents escalate into minor wars; and the lamps of civilization go dark.[32]

Despite the ravages of such an event, there is little probability that humans would be completely extinguished. A remnant would survive, and from their numbers civilization would begin to radiate. Ultimately, an event of such magnitude would have to be explained, for humans cannot endure without finding some meaning in their suffering. Explanations offered by the established traditions would not be seen as plausible, for against them would stand the plain fact that the old myths failed to prevent the most horrific event in human history. The most compelling stories in the aftermath of a global holocaust would be those explaining the event as a consequence of placing excessive and unsustainable demands on finite natural systems. These stories would explain that the holocaust happened because human beings, filled with supernatural pretensions, had failed to acknowledge and embrace their true status as contingent natural beings. In other words, the holocaust would be seen as a direct consequence of devaluing the order of nature. But nature, they will explain, is enough. It is the ultimate source of truth and value, the ultimate context for human fulfillment. To be wise is to live in harmony with nature.

If we are somehow spared the devastation of a global environmental holocaust, and if science education continues to improve and expand, then it is inevitable that the epic of cosmogenesis will come to play a decisive role in organizing the consciousness of men and women everywhere. And as this happens, the dynamics of cognitive dissonance will gradually create the conditions for religious naturalism to flourish. Cognitive dissonance—the state of holding incompatible beliefs or attitudes—is emotionally stressful for individuals, motivating them either to integrate the ideas or to reject one of them. I am persuaded—largely due to reports from students and colleagues over the years—that the epic of cosmogenesis nearly always prevails in cognitive contests with rival cosmologies. This means that traditional cultural myths will be forced to sacrifice many of their foundational beliefs in order to accommodate the scientific story. This process of accommodating scientific inquiry has been going on for centuries, of course, but it has accelerated during the past fifty years as the scientific story of creation has come more sharply into focus. The so-called battle between Darwin and the Bible is the final face-off between science and traditional Abrahamic cosmology, and this contest has been decisively called in Darwin's favor. It cannot be long before six-day creationists will be no more plentiful than flat-earthers.

The slow and steady scenario may be described as a closing of the supernaturalist gap between the natural and the sacred. This process is already under way. God, we may say, is gradually being naturalized, while nature is gradually being divinized. It may be premature to detect this process by the measures of the social sciences, but we can see it clearly in the personal stories of many individuals who have closed the gap from one direction or the other. Consider Gordon Kaufman, for example. Raised in a traditional midwestern Mennonite community, Kaufman pursued a theological career that can be charted as a gradual movement from traditional Christian belief to religious naturalism. He now envisions God as the creativity of the emerging cosmos.[33]

Or consider Stuart Kauffman, who closed the gap from the direction of science. Kauffman was raised in a nonobservant Jewish context and pursued a career in medicine and biochemistry, becoming one of the pioneers of emergence theory. Kauffman takes the grandeur of nature to heart, and while he never had any use for a transcendent creator, he regards the symbol of God to be uniquely powerful. In his 2008 book, *Reinventing the Sacred*, he advocates snatching the God symbol away from supernaturalists and using it (as Gordon Kaufman does) to describe emergent creativity:

> Is it, then, more amazing to think that an Abrahamic transcendent, omnipotent, omniscient God created everything around us, all that we participate in, in six days, or that it all arose with no transcendent Creator God, all on its own? I believe the latter is so stunning, so overwhelming, so worthy of awe, gratitude and respect, that it is God enough for many of us. God, a fully natural God, is the very creativity in the universe.[34]

Ursula Goodenough is another prominent religious naturalist who closed the gap from the direction of science. Goodenough was raised in a secular New Haven family and was trained as a cell biologist at Harvard. Her deep reverence for life was stimulated by her work as a research scientist, and she found she could not resist expressing her reverence in religious terms:

> And so, I profess my Faith. For me, the existence of all this complexity and awareness and intent and beauty, and my ability to apprehend it, serves as the ultimate meaning and the ultimate value. The continuation of life reaches around, grabs its own tail, and forms a sacred circle that requires no further justification, no Creator, no superordinate meaning of meaning, no purpose other than that the continuation continue until the sun collapses or the final meteor collides. I confess a credo of continuation.[35]

Chet Raymo offloaded his supernaturalist orientation when his encounters with philosophy and science left him in a state of cognitive dissonance. He pursued a career in physics, but never lost the deep sense of spiritual longing instilled in him by his Roman Catholic upbringing. For Raymo, God disappeared but the sacred remains:

> But there is something called natural religion (or, if you prefer, religious naturalism), that hides behind and within traditional faiths, and I am not so ready as Dawkins to

surrender a venerable and evocative language of praise to traditional theists. I will continue to pray, if by prayer you understand me to mean attention to the world. And I will try to live—as my Roman Catholic teachers urged me to live—in a state of grace. Not supernatural grace, to be sure, but the myriad natural graces that bless and hallow the everyday.[36]

Karl Peters had a religious experience as a young man and became an evangelical fundamentalist, filled with a call to enter the Christian ministry. By his second year in graduate school, however, he discovered that he had become an atheist (more cognitive dissonance). Peters's career as a philosopher of religion can be described as an impassioned quest to find a way of closing the gap between spiritual sensibilities and the scientific worldview. The gap was closed by his apprehension of the sacred as the creativity inherent in the natural order:

As long as we think of God as some kind of being, we will have difficulty perceiving God in the midst of our lives. . . . However, if we think of the word "God" more as a verb, then we can say that God equals creating; God is the process of creation, the event of creation.[37]

Donald Crosby opens his book, *A Religion of Nature*, with a chapter entitled, "From God to Nature." Here he details his spiritual odyssey—not unlike Karl Peters's story—from a ministry-bound Calvinist Christian to a pious non-theistic religious naturalist. The odyssey reads like a textbook study of cognitive dissonance. Crosby's Christian faith eroded gradually over several years' worth of reflection on the problem of evil, the incoherence of anthropomorphic theism, and the implications of evolutionary theory and environmental problems. He concluded, finally, that the natural world is metaphysically ultimate, and if this is true, then nature must also be religiously ultimate.

This book . . . makes a sustained case for nature itself as a proper focus of religious commitment and concern. For nature . . . is religiously ultimate, that is, self-sustaining and requiring no explanation for its existence beyond itself. . . . This book urges us to grant to nature the kind of reverence, awe, love and devotion we in the West have formerly reserved for God.[38]

As stories such as these continue to multiply—as they surely will, given the science education factor—the presence of religious naturalism will become noticeable *within the precincts of established religious traditions*. This is the key to the gradualist scenario: the supernaturalism of received traditions will gradually give way to an environmentally sensitive and cosmogenesis-inspired form of religious naturalism. There are encouraging signs that this phenomenon is already with us. Among Unitarians, for example, there is an active enclave of religious naturalists, calling themselves Unitarian Universalist Religious Naturalists (UURN). On their Web site we read: "The natural world and its emergent manifestations in human creativity and community are the focus of our immersion, wonder, and reverence, and our common naturalist orientation generates our shared sense of place, gratitude and joy."[39] Granted, this is not the Southern Baptist Convention or the Assemblies of God, but it is something. Even more impressive is the missionary zeal of Michael Dowd and Connie Barlow, America's "evolutionary evangelists." Barlow and Dowd have committed their energies and talents to spreading the "great story" of cosmogenesis and religious naturalism. For nearly a decade they have lived an itinerant life, traveling around the country giving speeches and workshops in churches, colleges, summer camps, and community centers.[40]

Personal odysseys that close the gap between the natural and the sacred, as well as institutional initiatives that accommodate religious naturalists, will continue. The process will be slow, to be sure, but in time we will see the great religious traditions relinquish their supernatural moorings in a manner not unlike the way many of the world's great universities have transcended the religious identities of their origins.

My point has been that either the catastrophic or the gradualist scenario will bring about the conditions for religious naturalism to flourish. But there can be nothing worthwhile in the flourishing of any religious orientation for its own sake. If there is any promise in religious naturalism it must be found in its potential for advancing the twin telē of personal wholeness and social coherence. The first of these goals is met by the potential for religious naturalism to enable individuals to achieve integrity and meaning in their lives. I hope it is evident by now that nature is enough to meet the challenges to personal wholeness.

Whether religious naturalism has the promise to advance the goal of social coherence is far more difficult to say. Opponents of religious naturalism are prepared to argue that it is a negative and divisive influence, not a constructive one. There may be a measure of substance to such arguments, but only in relation to very immediate and local circumstances. Advocates for religious naturalism will be quick to respond that it is precisely a myopic human concern for the immediate and local that has fueled the environmental crisis that now threatens viability for every species of life well beyond the immediate future. They will argue that there is no promise for the future of the biosphere apart from a story that can inform us about how things really are in the physical world, and which things ultimately matter for sustaining the viability of natural and social systems. We have no hope, they will plead, apart from a story that can unite diverse cultures with a vision of their shared natural history, their shared problems and their common destiny. We shall be doomed, they warn, unless we embrace a story that can move us to enlarge the scope of our interests and affections to include all humans, all species of life, and the biosphere itself. And no story, they will conclude, holds more promise for addressing these needs than the myth of religious naturalism.

5

Confessions of a
Religious Naturalist

The danger inherent in any disclosure of a personal creed is that it might be rendered obsolete overnight. This, at least, is the way seekers like to think about the spiritual life—and I fancy myself a seeker.

What do I seek? All the usual high-minded items: truth, wisdom, serenity, fulfillment, self-understanding, justice, a meaningful existence, the aboutness of everything. William James once remarked that the most interesting and important thing about a person was his or her view of life. This is what seekers are after: true and satisfying ways to think about what in life is most important to think about. Seeking is a vague enterprise.

How do I seek these things? Not very effectively, I fear to say, and not at all systematically. Seeking is not a discipline, it is a disposition of openness to the world of experience—one's own and, so far as possible, the experience of others. Like many seekers—by no means all—I have found the repositories of philosophical and religious reflection to be important resources for my own explorations. My attraction to these subjects is no doubt a function of my own background. I was raised in the Midwest by third-generation Norwegian immigrants. My parents both came from farming families, but left the farm—common among their generation—to take advantage of educational opportunities. My father became a Lutheran pastor, and my mother was trained in a teacher's college and, later, in a Bible institute. Our family was a marinade of Lutheran piety.

My father passed away in his early forties, leaving my mother to raise four young children—I was five at the time—with no money. By a combination of sheer determination, hard work, good luck, and unwavering faith, she managed against all odds to keep the family intact and well provisioned. The Lutheran church was her most valuable resource, her lifeline, and without its support she would never have managed to carry on from day to day. The religious life was not a weekly outing for my family—it was daily, hourly, and deadly serious.

I now look back at this religious context with the same mix of feelings you might have when considering your childhood home, or your first schoolroom: profound gratitude tempered by the recognition that these things have nothing more to offer. I was in countless ways shaped by Norwegian American Lutheran pietism, for which I will always be grateful, but I am now as far from its manner of thinking as one can possibly get. Which, in some ways, may not be all that far. That is, in *substance* my beliefs and attitudes are light years away, but the *forms* of my seeking may be as old and as deep as my Lutheran heritage. The same puzzling logic is evident in the reflections of Chet Raymo, who professes to be an atheist, yet continues to think in the formal categories of a Roman Catholic. This dynamic will be evident in the present chapter as well, for it seems somehow natural for me to reflect on my development as a religious naturalist in terms that will be readily familiar to an old-fashioned Lutheran. I have therefore selected a series of themes that cover most of what I take to be operative in the religious life, and for each of these themes I will attempt to do two things: to explain how they functioned in my earlier life as a practicing supernaturalist Christian, and to explain how I now think about them as a religious naturalist.

God and Creation

As a youngster I was taught the traditional old-man-in-the-sky concept of God. God the Father was an all-powerful, all-knowing, beneficent, eternal, and invisible creator and sustainer of the world. He (!) was the ultimate explanation for every fact and the ultimate justification (or condemnation) for every value. God created and loved the world. He was everywhere and knew everything, even my deepest secrets. As a child I was never afraid of God, for how could one fear a being that kept you safe from all harm? My siblings and I were assured by our mother that God was especially protective toward children who had lost their earthly father, a thought that entered my mind nearly every day. If ever I needed to feel special I would consider that I was on God's list of favorites—and probably quite high on the list, too, in view of the fact that my father had been a pastor. There is no question in my mind that the traditional God served as a great comfort to me as a child. No matter how confusing things might get, I would be safe, my family would be safe, the entire creation would be safe. The really wonderful thing about having such a concept of God is that you have everything covered. You can fit God in to explain anything at all, and you can ask God to make the world perform pretty much as you want it to. It's exactly like having a magic lamp with an obliging genie in it.

The problem, of course, is that this is fantasy, pure and simple—and anyone who bothers to give it a few moments of serious thought knows this. But thinking about God critically can be uncomfortable, for a couple of reasons. For one thing, it can make you feel guilty if you have been taught that having faith in God is the highest of human virtues, and that having doubts about God makes you a bad person. And for another, having doubts about God creates cognitive dissonance of the most intense sort. Part of you wants the good old God to stay right where he is, on call whenever you need him. But another part of you knows that this God is a logical monstrosity that you have believed in for your own comfort and convenience. The tension is between what one *wants* and what one *knows*, between truth and comfort.

I find it difficult to be precise about when I started having doubts about God. I suspect that most children first have doubts about God round about the time they first have doubts about Santa Claus. This makes sense, because God and Santa Claus share many of the same magical attributes. The big difference is that doubts about Santa Claus are allowed to run full-course, whereas doubts about God are explained away. Where I grew up there was a lot of care given to settling doubts about God, but almost no intellectual investments were made for the sake of saving Santa Claus.

In any event, I cannot remember when I *didn't* have questions about God. When these arose I would simply ask my mother and she would give me satisfying answers. Inevitably, of course, there were times when her answers were incomplete, or when they didn't square with previous answers, or when they just failed to convince me. Much later I came to realize that in answering my God questions my mother had been practicing the ancient tradition of "apologetic theology," that is, the practice of explaining how the concept of God is completely consistent with whatever it was that came along to create doubts about it. Where I grew up the God concept was kept revitalized by apologetic theology, but the Santa Claus concept was left on its own to be devoured by doubt.

The moment eventually arrived when I quit bringing God questions to my mother and took them straight to books about philosophy, psychology, and theology. I found theology books especially fascinating, because here were religious people who dismissed the old-man-in-the-sky concept out of hand, and replaced it with carefully crafted abstract ways to think about God. Academic theology, it turned out, was a terrific resource for relieving me from spells of cognitive dissonance. At the end of the day, however, I concluded that even academic theology could not save God.

I reasoned that a person in my position was left with four options. The first option was to hold fast to the traditional concept of God and to devise ways to prevent myself from asking questions. Perhaps I could convince myself that perfectly good answers do exist, but that it would be too bothersome to go to all the effort of finding them out. Actually, I'm sure I never considered this a live option, but as I write this I fancy that, if I had, I would have rejected it (as I do now) as lazy, weak-minded, and intellectually dishonest.

The second option would be to keep the traditional concept and to load myself up with ad hoc qualifications that explained away my doubts. This is the apologetic theology option, which I entertained for a substantial period of time, until it became too burdensome. I compare this option to the possibility of developing an apologetic tradition for the sake of saving the Santa Claus concept. Saving Santa by introducing ad hoc hypotheses is a real option—consider how some families invest themselves in keeping the ruse going—but what could possibly make the effort worthwhile in the long run? Eventually, apologetic theology begins to look as tortured and foolhardy as trying to save a worn tire by continuing to patch up the patches. A lost cause, if ever there was one.

A third option would be to relinquish the traditional concept of God in favor of something much more abstract and subtle—a concept that emphasizes mystery, or makes use of metaphysical principles that put God well beyond the reach of empirical inquiry. For example, Rudolf Otto described God as *mysterium tremendum et fascinans,* and Paul Tillich defined God as "the ground of being." This strategy for saving the concept of God has the appearance of being highly effective, but upon close inspection it disappoints. The trouble is this: if you have a concrete conception of God (e.g., all-powerful, all-knowing, beneficent creator), then it lacks coherence and plausibility, but if you trade this in for a high abstraction (*mysterium tremendum,* or ground of being), then the concept becomes flimsy and unable to perform the real work of explanation and justification.

I have finally settled on the fourth option, which is to give up on the concept of God altogether. This includes giving up on the prospect of outfitting God with a naturalistic definition, such as "the creativity of the cosmos." I have no strong objection to this approach, except to say that I fail to see where it takes us. If the concept of God adds nothing to one's understanding or appreciation of the creativity of the cosmos, then why bother using it?

If this were a theological tribunal I would have to admit to being an atheist, although I must confess to a twinge of discomfort with this label. It's not because I harbor a residue of old-fashioned theism, but rather because there is so much opprobrium attached to the term. In common parlance atheists are grouped together with terrorists, murderers, and kidnappers—and this despite the fact that these offenses correlate more closely with theism than atheism. I much prefer the term *non-theist* to *atheist*, but I will gladly confess to atheism if you admit to being an atheist as well. The point here is that everybody is an atheist by someone's definition. The early Christians were accused of atheism, and Islam accuses all non-Muslims of being heretics and infidels. So there.

Being an atheist does not, however, preclude the possibility of being genuinely religious. Not taking a metaphysical fiction to heart does not mean that I take nothing to heart, or that I deny the sacred. As a religious naturalist, I take nature to heart and affirm the mystery and sanctity of creation. In my own reflections on these matters I have gathered a sense that the theistic distinction between creator and creation introduces an artificial and unattractive gap between the natural and the sacred, with the effect (for me, at least) of diminishing the value of creation. Theism suggests that the creation counts for nothing apart from God—without God matter is mere grunge. As a naturalist, and as a material being, I hope to be excused for taking offense at this outrageous idea.

It remains to say something about the place of worship in connection with the theme of God and Creation. All religious naturalists are united by a reverence for nature, but they are not united by any distinctive patterns for expressing their reverence. That is, there are no universal practices that might describe the worship life of all religious naturalists. In this respect religious naturalism is rather like Hinduism. Hindu traditions honor human diversity in the religious life by encouraging individuals to seek paths of piety that suit their own dispositions and temperaments. Intellectuals who are drawn to the contemplative life of study and reflection will practice the disciplines of *jnana yoga*; practical take-charge types who cannot sit still or withdraw from social activity will find the path of *karma yoga* more agreeable; and passionate, sensitive, and emotionally expressive individuals will find *bhakti yoga* most satisfying. Religious naturalism honors human diversity in the same way. Thus, some religious naturalists might be found barefoot in a forest clearing, holding hands in a circle and singing praises to unspoiled wilderness. But others may be found alone, in urban libraries or laboratories, deepening their understanding and appreciation for some particular feature of the natural world. Yet others will be found expressing their reverence for nature by sitting in endless subcommittee meetings hammering out resolutions and legislative proposals. Nature, let us not forget, is everything and everywhere, spoiled and unspoiled by human activity. What matters most for the worship life of religious naturalists is imagination and experimentation.

As a child I attended worship services with unfailing regularity. I even sang in the choir and lit candles. However, with the exception of the music—at which Lutherans excel—I never found going to church worthwhile. Unlike Chet Raymo, whose atheistic soul is still moved by the pomp and ceremony of the mass, I found the worship life of my childhood to be boring. It must be said that the designers of the Lutheran worship service were finders, not seekers. The woodgrain patterns in the ancient oak pews held my attention more than anything else.

If I were a Hindu I would probably follow the path of *jnana yoga*, the path of contemplation. What I seek, primarily, is the stimulation of wonder and insight, which for me amounts to a lot of solitary reflection. I live on the banks of a lovely river, offering me a sort of sanctuary where I occasionally find opportunities for what might be called, very loosely, worship or meditation. There is nothing resembling discipline in these reflective events: I merely sit and gaze, usually at the flickering flames of a campfire or the rippling patterns of the water. Once I become relaxed my mind spontaneously wanders into the realms of the very large and the very small. I consider the size and the age of the universe, the billions of galaxies drifting aimlessly apart, and the billions of stars in each galaxy. I consider the history of our own star, circled by careless obedient planets. And then the Earth, with its abundant materials continuously recycling themselves. How many Earth-like planets are there in the universe? How unlikely is it to find places like this, capable of generating and supporting life? How many events, what sorts of events, had to take place before the emergence of life became possible? How close can I get to comprehending the fact that trillions of lifeless molecules—each one a universe in itself—are generating the life I now feel? What would the complete history of any particular atom look like? Eventually I am brought back to the middle realm, to my own body and the campfire. Here is an event—a relation between a living system and a pile of logs, both generating heat, both burning up. How did such an event come to be? What if it hadn't? How will this event change things?

I have discovered that these reflective occasions always have a renewing, refreshing effect on me. I have discovered that they invariably alter my attitudes and my perspective on the events of the day. And on very rare occasions, when the realms of the very large and the very small are brought together in a fleeting thought, I have discovered that it is possible to feel embraced by nature.

Sin and Grace

Imagine this: a sheriff bursts into a hospital delivery room and arrests a newborn infant. Moments later the infant is hauled into a courtroom, placed on trial, convicted, and sentenced to death. The crime? *Being born!* Welcome to the world of Lutheran theology.

At the core of Norwegian Lutheran pietism is the grunge theory of humanity. Humans aren't much, they are nothing but grunge, all the way through. Human beings are sinful creatures—in fact, they are *originally* sinful, conceived in sin, born into sin, and destined to lead sinful lives. To grow up Lutheran is to inherit a heavy burden of guilt. I hasten to add that the original sin of humankind is only half the story. The other half is that God has bestowed his grace on the faithful, thereby dropping the charges. The official theological formula is this: *simul justus et peccator* (likewise guilty and acquitted).

We had devotions at the dinner table every evening when I was growing up. This consisted of a reading from the Bible, followed by an illustrative story, and then punctuated by a prayer, the length of which was a precise measure of my mother's energy level. The theme of her prayers was always the same: *Lord, we are sinful creatures and deserve eternal damnation, but we beseech thee to be gracious unto us.* Sin and grace were drilled into us each day. It could have been a lot worse, however, and for many of my Lutheran friends it was. My mother, at least, had the sagacity to emphasize the grace as much as the sin, and she was careful to stress the point that we shouldn't take our guilt personally—it was inherited, ultimately, from Adam and Eve.

Again, I cannot be precise about the timing, but I managed to chuck the whole doctrine of original sin at a fairly early age. True, I grew up Lutheran, but I also grew up in the United States, where the legal system does not prosecute non-offenders. In America, Adam and Eve would have to bear the entire burden of sin on their own. But quite apart from legal principles, the whole idea of hereditary guilt appeared bogus to me. Inheriting the shape of one's nose or the color of one's hair made good sense, but how could one inherit irresponsibility? Critical questions about the doctrine of original sin have been commonplace in the history of Christian thought. The problem always centered on the mechanics of inheritance. Some theologians used the image of a metaphysical stain on the souls of newborn children, while others tried to biologize guilt by putting it into the germ line. But I wasn't buying any of it.

Many years later, however, I came to realize that the doctrine of original sin expressed a hugely important insight about human nature, despite the fact that it was couched in unacceptable metaphysical terms. The insight is that human beings cannot avoid breaking rules—no matter how hard we try, it is inevitable that we will goof up. The reason for this is not that we are evil or sinful by nature, but rather because we are governed by a plurality of motivational systems that inevitably conflict with one another. Our physiological drive systems urge us to eat when hungry and to keep ourselves warm and dry. Seeking nourishment and warmth are the "goods" scripted into our nature. But suppose you are fiercely hungry and the only way to get food is to go out into the freezing rain and fetch it. There is no possible way to achieve both goods, and one has to be sacrificed for the sake of the other. Here's another simple illustration. John and Julie both come to you asking for your last morsel of food. You happen to be grateful to John for a recent favor, but Julie's hunger is noticeably more acute. This leaves you torn between gratitude and sympathy, unable to satisfy both emotional mandates. To be human means to be faced with difficult choices like these on a daily basis, making it impossible to achieve good and avoid evil in every case. We are destined to sin.

But consider how much more complicated matters became after the great leap forward, when our ancestors introduced articulate moral systems. Then, in addition to the intuitive morality of our several inherited motivational systems, we became burdened with counter-intuitive rules that had to be learned and remembered. The business of good and evil suddenly transcended the simple mechanics of gut reactions to require deliberate judgments involving moral principles. In the great leap forward our ancestors discovered a whole new logic of morality, a discovery perhaps not unlike the one in the Bible where Adam and Eve discovered the tree of the knowledge of good and evil.

Having articulate rules to manage makes it even more certain that we will goof up along the way.

Once we naturalize the doctrine of original sin we can see that it represents a perfectly sound insight about human nature. But the other half of the story has to do with God's grace. Is there a place for this doctrine in a religious naturalist outlook? I believe there is. We have already seen that every post-campsite human society needs to invent and enforce articulate rules. The alternative is to default into campsite sociality. And we have seen that when a learned moral system is added to our inherited plurality of motivational systems it becomes impossible for any human to achieve moral perfection. We all sin, by necessity. But there is one additional thing that every social group must provide, namely, the means whereby rule offenders can be restored to their original status as full members of the social order. That is, in addition to moral rules, every society must provide a moral reset button.

The Christian doctrine of sin and grace says that we are all judged guilty by the Law, and consequently we all deserve to be damned. But God, in his grace, gives us another chance to live a righteous life. Grace is construed as an undeserved benefit. Moral offenders do not deserve rewards, but they get off the hook anyway. Now, there is nothing even slightly unique about the Christian doctrine of grace—it is a culturally specific way of articulating a dynamic of moral restitution that is characteristic of every stable social order. Think about it: everybody comes up sooner or later as a moral offender and deserves to be called on the carpet or put on the hook. Along with this comes social scorn and a psychological burden of guilt. But what are the chances that a social group might continue to function harmoniously when, first of all, everyone feels guilty and, secondly, everybody is holding a grudge against everybody else? Without a moral reset button, without the dynamics of forgiveness, societies become dysfunctional in a hurry. Obviously, moral offenses vary in gravity, and there are some extreme cases where moral restitution appears out of the question. But these are the exceptions to the general dynamics of blame and forgiveness that characterize every functional social system.

I have completely rejected the doctrines of sin and grace as functions of God's judgment and mercy, but naturalized versions of these doctrines occupy a central place in my understanding of religious naturalism. In practical terms, I would like to think that naturalizing sin and grace can help to make one a more understanding and forgiving person. When you realize that everyone is geared up in a way that makes them vulnerable to goofing up on a fairly regular basis, then you may find yourself just a bit more inclined to lighten up and cut your neighbor some slack. Most people, most of the time, are simply trying to do their best. And if I can manage to be more forgiving, then there is a good chance that others in my acquaintance might reciprocate.

There is one further aspect of the doctrine of grace that strikes me as appropriate to religious naturalism. Here I mean the many natural graces that we heard Chet Raymo refer to in the previous chapter. If grace is understood as unwarranted benefit, then it certainly is the case that nature is full of grace. I have done nothing to deserve the air I breathe or the soil and waters that produce the food I eat. I have done nothing to deserve the energy that I exploit from the sun or the endless services rendered by the earth's decomposers. These, and so much more, come to me as the free gifts of nature, and I would take a low view of myself if ever I failed to be grateful for them, or if I failed to act in ways befitting my gratitude.

Evil and Suffering

Martin Luther was not one to take evil lightly—legend has it that he once threw his ink pot at the devil. He took suffering seriously as well, citing the Book of Job among his favorite books of the Bible, second only to St. Paul's Letter to the Romans. If anything, Norwegian Lutheran pietism takes evil and suffering even more seriously than Luther did. If you doubt this, you might try sampling a few Scandinavian films. Religious traditions take suffering seriously because all humans experience suffering and seek explanations for it. The principle seems to be that suffering is tolerable if it can be rendered meaningful. It becomes problematic only when it appears pointless.

The Lutheran tradition of my childhood bought into the standard Christian explanation for evil and suffering. Humans were created as free moral agents who were expected to use their freedom in serving God's will. Suffering entered the picture when Adam and Eve succumbed to evil and misused their freedom. Humans suffer, therefore, because humans sin. We sinful Lutherans were taught that we deserved all the suffering we happened to get. That was supposed to make it tolerable. There are occasions, to be sure, when this explanation appears to fail. In the Book of Job, for example, we have an apparently righteous man who endures extreme suffering. But if Job was indeed sinless, then what was the point of his suffering? Here we are given a backup explanation: God allows us to suffer as a way of testing our faith. Presumably, there is a correlation between one's faith and one's tolerance for adversity, so that a dose of misfortune will smoke out those of inferior piety. We were never told why an omniscient God would find such experiments necessary. On those occasions when the backup explanation failed to convince, there was always the trump card: God's allowance of suffering is ultimately mysterious, but in the fullness of time all will be revealed, and then the faithful will be rewarded for their patience and their trust in God's mercy.

The Christian tradition has been forced to spend a lot of intellectual energy answering the challenge of the infamous problem of evil. The problem arises for many theistic traditions because they advance the claim that the universe is a moral order. If this claim were dropped, as it is by most religious naturalists, then the problem goes away. The classical problem of evil can be simply stated in the following argument:

1. If an all-powerful, all-knowing, and beneficent God exists, then there would be no unnecessary evil or pointless suffering in the world.

2. But there are instances of unnecessary evil and pointless suffering in the world.

3. Therefore, it is not the case that an all-powerful, all-knowing, beneficent God exists.

There are basically six options for making this problem go away:

1. Deny the existence of God

2. Deny the reality of evil

3. Modify the divine attributes

4. Reject the relevance of logic in theological matters

5. Theodicy (justification of God)

6. The mystery defense

The first option accepts atheism; the second option takes a nonrealist approach to values (which seems to imply that the universe is not a moral order); the third option essentially accepts the argument, but reinstates God with reduced attributes; and the fourth option merely asserts that the argument is unfair. Most of the theological attention has focused on the fifth and sixth options. "Theodicy" (Greek: *theos*

+ *dike*) means "justification of God." The strategy here is to argue that what may *appear* to be unnecessary evil or pointless suffering really isn't unnecessary or pointless. God allows evil and suffering, but he does not do so without good reason. Theodicy, then, attempts to demonstrate that every case of apparently pointless suffering has its point in relation to a greater good. By analogy: abdominal surgery may entail suffering, but the suffering is necessary for the achievement of a greater good (restored health). If a theodicy succeeds, then the problem of evil is explained away. The mystery defense is the trump card mentioned earlier. It doesn't even try to explain away apparently pointless suffering.

This is not the occasion to evaluate theological attempts to save the concept of God from the problem of evil. I will only say that in my judgment none of them succeeds, leaving the first option as the most reasonable. But the focus here should be on what religious naturalism has to say about evil and the experience of suffering. It will come as no surprise when I say that naturalists address the phenomena of evil and suffering by naturalizing them. The story goes as follows. Organisms are variously equipped by natural selection with mechanisms for detecting sources of benefit and harm in their environments, enabling them to take measures either to advance or to safeguard their viability. These mechanisms and the arousals they cause—either pleasurable or painful—are demonstrably adaptive. A squirrel unable to experience fear or a child unable to feel pain would both be seriously disadvantaged.

Suffering is therefore biologically pointful: it increases prospects for reproductive fitness. It is certainly true, however, that naturalism cannot specify the biological pointfulness of all instances of suffering. Chronic pain, for example, and phantom limb pain, are dysfunctional conditions affecting detection systems, as are poor eyesight or deafness. The point is that for naturalists suffering—even dysfunctional or pointless suffering—does not call for a moral explanation, as it does for theists. If the universe is not a moral order, then the moral integrity of the universe cannot be called into question by the existence of suffering. To naturalize suffering is to neutralize the problem of evil.

None of this suggests that religious naturalists are indifferent about suffering or deny that suffering has moral implications. It is merely to say that the moral challenge of suffering is not to justify it but to *use* it. The most important thing about suffering is that it gives us information about the states of natural and social systems. The information is often costly—physical and emotional distress are difficult to bear—but most of the time, and in the long run, it is worth the expense.

Interpreting information provided by suffering can amount to an extremely complex process. For example, suppose Mary is suffering the symptoms of a respiratory infection. Her suffering tells us that she, an individual organism, is distressed and in need of a particular form of therapy. But Mary's suffering might also alert us to a pollution problem in her neighborhood, informing us about distress in a natural ecosystem, calling for some form of ecotherapy. The ecological distress might in turn alert us to certain deficiencies in social systems—say, overpopulation or underlegislation—that call for political remediation. Suffering is rarely as localized as it first appears.

My kind of religious naturalism sees all moral activity in terms of therapy and politics, that is, actions that bear upon the integrity of natural and social systems. With respect to humans, therapy and politics consist of the strategies we employ in our efforts to achieve personal wholeness and social coherence. Suffering, on this view, provides essential information in directing our therapeutic and political responses to it in our pursuit of viability.

I now want to suggest that there is another, deeper sense in which suffering may be used—a sense that is more compatible with traditional religious discourse about it. What I mean is that suffering may be used as a transformative factor in a person's life. It has a way of changing people, sometimes for better and sometimes for worse.

We commonly think of suffering as a private and subjective phenomenon, but nothing could be farther from the truth. True, no one but you can actually experience your suffering, but the manner of your coping with suffering radiates all over the place. Consider: an excruciating toothache might make a person irritable and edgy, predisposed to treating family members severely, causing them emotional distress, and perhaps even damaging family relations beyond repair, leading to a breakdown of family solidarity. By contrast, some individuals cope with suffering in ways that are personally and socially constructive. Bearing up under distress with courage and without complaint will often win the admiration and sympathetic cooperation of others.

The manner in which individuals respond to suffering is not well understood. Some persons become deeply embittered, resentful, impatient, demanding, cynical, and fearful, while others become more sensitive, more compassionate, more understanding, more focused, and more courageous. Suffering has the potential for robbing persons of their sense of a meaningful life, perhaps because the pursuits that have made life meaningful are no longer possible. But suffering also has the potential to prompt individuals to reexamine their lives, to reorder their priorities and to embrace more meaningful goals.

At the beginning of the previous chapter I suggested that one of the principal functions of religious traditions is to promote personal wholeness, and it is evident that personal wholeness is seldom more fragile than when a person is faced with suffering and loss. Religious traditions have therefore developed resources for helping individuals to cope with suffering constructively, and even to use suffering as an occasion for self-transformation and a more meaningful existence. It is often assumed that supernaturalist religious beliefs (e.g., a divine purpose, cosmic justice) are exclusively effective in helping people to bear suffering constructively. I would not doubt for a moment that supernaturalist beliefs often do ease the burden of suffering, but it is simply not true that such beliefs are uniquely valuable for coping. The world is too full of examples of supernaturalists who cannot bear suffering gracefully, and naturalists who can.

Our question must now be this: What does religious naturalism have to offer to individuals faced with intense suffering? As there is no broadly established doctrine of suffering among religious naturalists, I am left to speak for myself. In my life so far I have faced occasional instances of suffering and loss, but I have never had to endure extreme and pointless suffering. I have been spared "the big one," whatever that might turn out to be. But when I am brought to face the big one this is what I hope for myself . . .

I will find it comforting to know that there is no moral judgment behind it all—that I am not being made to suffer because I am a bad person. I will remind myself that suffering—often intense—is a universal human experience, and the meager price we must all pay for the priceless joys of sentience. I will draw strength from examples of heroic suffering: from the innocent Jesus, who forgave his executioners, and from Nelson Mandela who, after twenty-seven years as a political prisoner, honored his jailers at his presidential inauguration. I will be mindful that those I love will be deeply affected by my response to adversity. It will be within my power to comfort and inspire them with an example of courage and serenity. I will know that my response will equip them to face their own big ones. And I will know that in my suffering I become an exemplar of nature itself—that my suffering embodies the deep truth that cosmogenesis is a creative spectacle of struggle and strife.

Death and Salvation

My siblings and I were forced to come to terms with death at a very early age. The terms were that our father had been "called home to glory" by God, and that we would join him in heaven if we remained faithful. It would be the most joyous reunion imaginable. My mother, who remained a widow for the next twenty-two years, kept the death recent and the reunion imminent with daily references to both events. Death and salvation were not occasional subjects in our home. Nor were they ever separated. In my young mind they were synonymous. I cannot recall ever having the slightest fear of death. What's to fear about the most joyous reunion ever?

I never feared death, but I had lots of questions about it, which my mother always took care to answer with an air of confidence and anticipation. At some—again, obscure—point in time I started to entertain questions about heaven that I sensed would not be welcomed, so I kept them to myself. In particular, there were two insoluble problems that kept returning to me. The first was what I now call "the dilemma of charitable homicide," and it went like this. My early Christian education included, among other items, two important principles. One was that good Christians should be prepared to make sacrifices for the welfare of others, and the second was that eternal life in heaven would be far better than life on earth. Occasionally, when I put these principles together, I came up with the conclusion that I should murder my brother. Sending my brother to heaven would be the greatest imaginable thing I could do for him. True, I would sacrifice my own salvation in the process, but the Christian life was ultimately all about sacrifice anyway. The logic of this argument impressed me as unassailable, yet I resisted the urge to act on it because the conclusion seemed just too counterintuitive.

The other problem concerned the heavenly reunion with my father. We were taught that bodies went to the grave and souls went to heaven. The great reunion, then, would be a reunion of souls. At some point I started to have concerns about how my father and I would recognize each other in heaven. And beyond that, there were problems about communication—if we didn't have bodies, then we wouldn't have voices or ears. And even beyond that, there was this problem: if our souls communicated somehow directly, then how could my father distinguish between genuine messages from me and mere hallucinations of such messages?

These two childish concerns became the least of my problems once I started bringing my questions to books. In the course of time and study, my supernaturalist beliefs about death and salvation were displaced entirely by naturalist beliefs. Interestingly, I have remained fearless about death. I am perfectly willing to attribute this fortunate fact to my early religious education, but I am also aware that it has no bearing on the truth of my early beliefs. My present beliefs about death are typical of materialistic naturalism. Immortal souls, I believe, do not exist, and when the body dies the person (the self) will be annihilated. Just as we did not exist a thousand years before our birth, so we shall not exist beyond our death. Each self is a momentary blip in the vast universal stretch of space-time.

I have come to believe that death is implicit in the process of life itself. It is quite natural to think about death as a problem. Indeed, in most cultural traditions death is *the* problem of human existence. But from the perspective of evolutionary wisdom death is not a problem at all, it is a *solution*—and a fairly recent one at that. Prior to the invention of sexual reproduction there was nothing inevitable about death. It happened all the time, of course, but it did not need to. Many species of organisms need never to die. Single-cell organisms reproduce by simply dividing into halves, each half becoming a distinct individual capable of further subdivision. Death is not a part of the picture, as both halves go on living, enjoying a virtual immortality. Death has no sting to an amoeba.

It is only among sexually reproducing multicellular organisms that death enters the picture as a certainty. The reason has to do with the divergence of cells into the germ line and soma lines. The germ line (reproductive cells) produces informed seed for the next generation, while the many soma lines diverge for the production of various body parts. The body negotiates the environment, thus enabling the germ line to do its own job of bringing forth more seed-bearing organisms. The strategy is simple and elegant: the soma lines are instruments of the germ line. Having performed its duty to the germ line, the body becomes redundant and eventually dies, making room for the next generation. But the germ line continues immortally onward in subsequent generations. The death of the body is an essential part of the design.

In the wisdom of this scheme it becomes difficult to view death in a negative sense. The inevitability of my death is now held to be a necessary condition for the life I now have—a mere entrance fee, to be paid on the way out. If there were no death there would be no soma lines, and without soma lines there would be no possibility of an embodied person—no memories, no loves, no joys, no wonder or wisdom, no longing or learning. These are among the splendors of the body, and for these we must die. We *must* die because we *get to* live. To the extent that I cherish my life, therefore, I have reason to be profoundly grateful for my death. When I have occasion to mourn the death of others I will try to absorb the loss in what I have gained from them. I will try to understand my grief as a measure of my gratitude.

And when I have occasion to consider the fact of my own death I will attempt to think large. I will try to see that a soma-centered story of the self is a small and impoverished view, and that the life within me was first quickened among the primordial organisms appearing on earth nearly four billion years ago. I will affirm that all lives, no less my own, are instruments of life itself. And by these measures I will submerge the absurdity of death in gratitude for the wonder and wisdom of life.

John Haught has been particularly harsh with religious naturalists on the subject of death and immortality. He believes naturalism implies a bleak and depressing view that can never satisfy our inherent longing for immortality. The attempts of "sunny" religious naturalists to smile in the face of death amount to nothing more than self-deception. Haught's intolerance of naturalist views on death and immortality relies on two assumptions that naturalism finds unacceptable. The first assumption is that the value of something is in some way relative to its duration, so that the naturalist's claim that the self is a temporary phenomenon is taken by Haught to imply a devaluation of human life. Christian doctrine, by contrast, grants immortality to the self, which seems to imply a higher valuation of human life. This line of reasoning is lost on naturalists, who are likely to be amused by the implications of coupling value to duration. An infection that lasts for eight weeks is better than one lasting for three days?

The other assumption isn't any better. Haught rather blithely assumes that where there's a will there's a way. That is, if humans have certain inherent longings, then they must be satisfiable in reality. Naturalism cannot satisfy our longings for immortality, so it must be an unsatisfying view. And if it is unsatisfying, that is reason enough to reject it. By contrast, we have good reason to accept the doctrine of immortality because it satisfies our longings. The fallacy here is to accept human *wants* as criteria for judging *truth*. The consequences of using desire as a substitute for evidence can be devastating. The Bush White House, for example, came to believe that Iraq possessed weapons of mass destruction because they wanted it to be true. Haught's rejection of religious naturalism for the reason that it fails to satisfy a desire for eternal life plays directly into the hands of the old Freudian argument that religion amounts to a childish form of wish-fulfillment.

And while we're on the subject we might ask whether Haught is too hasty in his claim that humans possess an inherent longing for eternal life. Presumably, he means that this longing is an evolved adaptive trait. Naturalists will not reject the notion that organisms are equipped with adaptations for self-maintenance, but they might well hesitate over the word *eternal*. This is clearly an extrapolation from the observation that organisms are designed with a telos for continuation. But are we designed to long for *eternal* continuation? Caregivers in nursing homes tell us that it is common for elderly and infirm individuals to give up their will to live at a certain point. Must we consider all of these many cases to be examples of malfunction? That's hard to say. At the very least we must agree that the inference from self-maintaining mechanisms to a longing for eternal life is questionable.

But even if we allow the inference, it remains an open question whether eternal life in an obscure supernatural realm is something worth longing for. In order to answer such a question we would need a lot of very specific information about the conditions of the afterlife. But specific information about the afterlife is something we rarely get, and what we do get usually sounds ridiculous (streets of gold? eighty thousand servants and seventy-two virgins?). If the afterlife is ultimately desirable, then any coherent, general description of it will include the idea that in heaven all our desires will be satisfied. This seems to be what most people have vaguely in mind when the subject of heaven comes up. But if there is a social aspect to the afterlife, then this concept would be a recipe for utter chaos. Imagine a social order where every person always gets exactly what he or she wants! It would be sheer hell. Besides, how long would it take before we got bored with a hedonic Freudian paradise of this sort? The point here is that nobody has the faintest idea what they're talking about when they get onto the topic of an afterlife. And this being the case, no one should feel obligated to take such talk seriously.

Each distinctive religious tradition describes a spiritual destination and a path to its achievement. When substantial disagreements arise about the understanding of the destination, or the details of the pathway, then schisms are likely to appear, threatening to undermine the coherence of the tradition. Reform movements within religious traditions can almost invariably be traced to such disagreements. Within the Abrahamic traditions, Second Isaiah, St. Paul, and Martin Luther (among others) may be seen as visionary leaders of reform movements, each one finding fault with the way their received traditions understood the nature and mechanics of salvation. I have suggested that if we are spared a major global holocaust, then we are likely to see naturalistic reform movements taking shape within established religious traditions, offering a very different approach to salvation.

In my upbringing the ideas of death and salvation were so closely linked that they became effectively synonymous. Salvation was something that happened when a person died. Salvation was also understood to be a discrete, atomic process—it happened one soul at a time. The emergent religious naturalism of the future will find no place for either of these ideas. If the concept of salvation is to have any meaning at all for religious naturalists it must be something for the living, and it must include social systems. Salvation is molecular, not atomic.

Religious naturalism of the sort I envision will understand salvation in terms of safeguarding the life-giving potential of the biosphere. If there are synonyms for salvation they will be sustainability and viability. For humans in particular, salvation will be a matter of achieving personality and sociality simultaneously, which is what I meant by the molecular characteristic. We save individuals by enhancing the solidarity of their communities, and we save communities by nurturing and enabling their individual members. To succeed in achieving these twin telē is all the glory we shall ever need.

Faith, Hope, and Love

There is no supernaturalist lock on faith, hope, and love. Naturalists embody these virtues as well. For naturalists, however, faith cannot mean believing without evidence, hope cannot mean the prospect of overcoming death, and love cannot mean that we are unconditionally loved.

Imagine yourself a teacher with a pair of very persistent students to whom you have assigned a math problem. The first student comes with a wrong answer, and you say, "wrong answer, try again." But the student stubbornly continues to insist that the answer is correct, *despite* the fact of your judgment. The second student also comes with a wrong answer, and you say, "wrong answer, try again." So the student does try again, and again, and yet again, *despite* previous unsuccessful efforts. Here we are presented with two forms of faith: one continues to believe despite the evidence, and the other continues to inquire despite failures.

The religious tradition of my upbringing, sad to say, made a high virtue of the first form of faith. Martin Luther insisted that "scripture alone" was enough to certify the truth of Christian faith. In other words, the answer was itself the evidence. Luther also hated philosophical inquiry, calling reason "the devil's greatest whore." My mother followed Luther in this teaching, but my siblings and I were quick to notice that it was only in matters of religion that she refused to consider evidence. In every other domain of life she remained a strict evidential rationalist.

Religious naturalism has no place for faith as belief despite evidence. However, it considers the other form of faith—persistence in pursuit of truth—to be a mark of good character. I have come to regard this second form of faith as much more consistent with the deepest teachings of most religious traditions. At their best, all religions are life-affirming. Basically, they all admonish us to persist in living, to "keep on keepin' on," to pick ourselves up, dust ourselves off, and start all over again. I see this as the only plausible reading of the Christian story of crucifixion and resurrection: it's not over yet; there's more to come; defeat is not final; it's always darkest before dawn; you can do it. These familiar expressions take us to the heart of faith, to the credo of continuation, the essential algorithm of viability. Faith, for religious naturalism, echoes the slogan for a recent Harvard class reunion: "In spite of everything . . . Yes!"

Hope is what happens when one takes to heart the best possible future outcomes. It is important to distinguish sharply between hoping and wishing. Hope is always contingent on real possibilities, whereas wishing is not. You may wish that John McCain had won the election of 2008, but it makes no sense to hope for it. When your genie appears from the lamp you should consider the possibilities before you speak. Hope is contingent on what is possible, which means that genuine hope will always be well informed. To long for the continuation of life on earth beyond the death of our sun is to nurture a false hope. Likewise, you are hoping falsely if you look forward to having thoughts and experiences after the material of your brain has decomposed.

I was raised on a packet of false hopes—that I would live forever, that I would be reunited with my father, that I was special in the eyes of God. And I would be less than honest if I denied that losing these hopes was a painful and confusing process. But suffering and loss are often transformative: they have a way of clearing the air and opening one to the adventure of new insights and the exhilaration of a fresh perspective. Losing faith brings the promise of finding it.

Religious naturalists encourage genuine, informed hope. Like most people, they will hope to leave behind a world that is more just, more beautiful and more viable than the one they found. They hope that scientific inquiry will continue to advance, for in the process of learning they see heightened possibilities for achieving personal wholeness and social coherence. "Sunny" naturalists—the ones who take an emergence view of nature—may appear to be deluded to some observers because of their vague and sometimes speculative optimism about long-term future possibilities for life. But emergentists, you may recall, feel justified in their vague optimism because they are open to the prospects that possibilities can change radically. New relations impose new constraints, bringing new lawful possibilities into the picture. And when possibilities change miracles can happen. Religious naturalists cannot hope beyond the possibilities, but they may hope for new possibilities. And such hope—even vague, speculative hope—is what sustains faith.

I had the good fortune of growing up with a clear sense that I was loved unconditionally. God loved me and my mother loved me, and I was confident that they would go on loving me no matter what offenses I might commit—and I committed my share! But my mother has passed away, and God has vanished from my imagination, with the result that I no longer feel the sense of being loved unconditionally. But I do not feel diminished in any way by this loss—and I am trying to be as honest with myself as possible about this. I know that while my mother lived my siblings and I occupied the center of her universe of meaning, and I know that this is no longer the case. I miss my mother's presence, but somehow I don't miss being the cherished center of anyone's universe.

I strongly agree that the experience of being loved is critical for one's sense of personal fulfillment and self-esteem, but I am not convinced that feeling loved unconditionally is essential for personal wholeness, and in some ways it might even be counterproductive. To my mind, the capacity *to love unconditionally* is far more important for personal wholeness than *being loved* unconditionally. To love as God is presumed to love is more important than being loved by God. To love unconditionally is to love without regard for oneself, to invest oneself in goals and outcomes that have no bearing on one's own interests. Those who live for themselves alone have nothing much to live for. Genuinely to love another person is to take their interests to heart in ways that involve self-sacrifice. Genuinely to love peace and justice is to take them to heart in ways that relativize the self. My kind of religious naturalism—like all religious traditions at their best—seeks ways to inspire this self-transcending love.

With this I take my leave, confident in the assertion that—irrespective of your metaphysical commitments—if you are able to affirm life despite its defeats, and if you are open to radically new possibilities, and if you can manage to take to heart things more excellent, more beautiful and more sacred than yourself, then you know perfectly well that life is full of meaning.

Notes

Preface

1. John Haught, *Is Nature Enough?* (New York: Cambridge University Press, 2006).

Chapter 1. Introduction

1. Ludwig Wittgenstein, *Tractatus Logico-Philosophicus*, trans. C. K. Ogden (London: Routledge and Kegan Paul, 1981), §6.521.

2. *Der Muselmann* (literally, "muslim") means "one who submits." The term was applied to the class of prisoners who eventually gave up any interest in living, even to the point of lacking the motivation to commit suicide. *Der Muselmann* was the most commonly used term, but in some camps the same class of prisoners (the living dead) was known as "cretins," "donkeys," "cripples," "swimmers," or "trinkets." See Wolfgang Skofsky, *The Order of Terror: The Concentration Camp*, trans. William Templer (Princeton: Princeton University Press: 1997).

3. Jean Amery, *At the Mind's Limits* (New York: Shocken Books, 1998), 9.

4. Zdzislaw Ryn and Stanislav Klodzinski, "At the Borderline Between Life and Death," in *Auschwitz-Hefte* (Basel: Beltz, 1987), 1:128–29.

5. See Martin Davis, "The Philosophy of Mind," in *Philosophy*, ed. A. C. Grayling (New York: Oxford University Press, 1995), 275–80.

6. Fyodor Dostoyevsky, *The Brothers Karamazov*, trans. Constance Garnett (New York: W. W. Norton, 1976), 244.

7. Christopher Belshaw, *Ten Good Questions About Life and Death* (Oxford: Blackwell Publishing, 2005), 115.

8. Thomas Nagel, "The Absurd," in *The Meaning of Life*, ed. E. D. Klemke (New York: Oxford University Press, 2000), 176–85.

Chapter 2. The Reality of Meaning

1. Scott Atran, *In Gods We Trust* (New York: Oxford University Press, 2002), 60.

2. Aristotle, *Nicomachean Ethics*, trans. Martin Ostwald (New York: Bobbs-Merrill, 1962), 291.

3. René Descartes, *The Philosophical Writings of Descartes*, trans. John Cottingham, Robert Stoothoff, and Dugald Murdoch (Cambridge: Cambridge University Press, 1988), 1:381–84.

4. The principal sources for Whitehead's metaphysical views are: A. N. Whitehead, *Process and Reality* (New York: Free Press, 1978) and A. N. Whitehead, *Science and the Modern World* (New York: Free Press, 1967).

5. Søren Kierkegaard, *Fear and Trembling*, trans. Walter Lowrie (Princeton: Princeton University Press, 1941).

6. Søren Kierkegaard, *Concluding Unscientific Postscript to Philosophical Fragments*, trans. H. V. Hong and E. H. Hong (Princeton: Princeton University Press, 1992).

7. Jean-Paul Sartre, "Existentialism Is a Humanism," in *Existentialism From Dostoevsky to Sartre*, ed. Walter Kaufman (New York: Meridian Books, 1956), 288–311.

8. Richard Rorty, *Contingency, Irony, and Solidarity* (New York: Cambridge University Press, 1989), xiv.

9. W. K. C. Guthrie, *The Presocratic Tradition From Parmenides to Democritus* (Cambridge: Cambridge University Press, 1965), ch. 8.

10. Thomas Hobbes, *Leviathan*, (London: Penguin Books, 1968).

11. Paul M. Churchland, "Eliminative Materialism and the Propositional Attitudes," *The Journal of Philosophy* 78:2 (1981): 76.

Chapter 3. The Emergence of Meaning

1. John Haught, *Is Nature Enough?* (New York: Cambridge University Press, 2006), 80.

2. Steven Weinberg, *The First Three Minutes* (New York: Basic Books, 1977).

3. Robert Wright, *Non-Zero* (New York: Pantheon, 2000).

4. Deacon, Terrence, *The Symbolic Species* (New York: W. W. Norton and Company, 1997), 364.

5. Steven Pinker, *The Blank Slate* (New York: Viking, 2002).

6. Rorty, *Contingency, Irony, and Solidarity*, 92–93.

7. Terrence Deacon, "Emergence: The Hole at the Wheel's Hub," in *The Re-Emergence of Emergence*, ed. Philip Clayton and Paul Davies (New York: Oxford University Press, 2006), 137.

8. Loyal Rue, *Everybody's Story* (Albany: State University of New York Press, 1999), xii.

Chapter 4. Religion Naturalized, Nature Sanctified

1. Isaiah, 44:14–21 (The New English Bible).

2. The theory of religion summarized in this section is more fully presented in my previous book, *Religion Is Not About God* (New Brunswick: Rutgers University Press, 2005).

3. Mircea Eliade, *The Sacred and the Profane* (New York: Harcourt, Brace and World, 1957).

4. G. E. Moore, *Principia Ethica* (Cambridge: Cambridge University Press, 1903).

5. Moore himself is famous for pulling a similar stunt on the proponents of radical skepticism ("the Moorean Shift").

6. Pinker, *The Blank Slate*.

7. Donald Crosby, *A Religion of Nature* (Albany: State University of New York Press, 2002), 169.

8. Brian Swimme, "Cosmogenesis," in *Worldviews and Ecology,* ed. Mary Evelyn Tucker and John Grim (Maryknoll, NY: Orbis Books, 1994), 239.

9. Joanna Macy, "Our Life as Gaia," in *Thinking Like a Mountain,* ed. John Seed and Joanna Macy (East Haven, CT: New Society Publishers, 1988), 57–60.

10. Haught, *Is Nature Enough?*, 9.

11. Ibid., 96, 140–42, 205.

12. Ibid., 14, 18, 28.

13. Ibid., 19–20, 96.

14. Ibid., 16–18.

15. Ibid., 30–31.

16. Ibid., 22.

17. Ibid., 179.

18. Ibid., 63–65.

19. Ibid., 7, 80, 82, 111, 127, 131–37, 142.

20. Ibid., 35.

21. Ibid., 36.

22. Ibid., 115.

23. Ibid., 68, 131, 135, 212.

24. Ibid., 137.

25. See above, p. 25.

26. Haught, *Is Nature Enough?,* 22.

27. Ibid., 21.

28. Ibid., 10.

29. Steven Weinberg, *Dreams of a Final Theory* (New York: Pantheon Books, 1992), 256.

30. Haught, *Is Nature Enough?*, 194.

31. World Pantheist Movement. http://www.pantheism.net/.

32. Rue, *Religion Is Not About God,* 360.

33. Gordon Kaufman, *In the Beginning . . . Creativity* (Minneapolis: Augsburg Fortress, 2004).

34. Stuart Kauffman, *Reinventing the Sacred* (New York: Basic Books, 2008), 6.

35. Ursula Goodenough, *The Sacred Depths of Nature* (New York: Oxford University Press, 1998), 171.

36. Chet Raymo, *When God Is Gone Everything Is Holy* (Notre Dame, IN: Sorin Books, 2008), 19.

37. Karl Peters, *Dancing with the Sacred* (Harrisburg, PA: Trinity Press, 2002), 39.

38. Crosby, *A Religion of Nature*, xi.

39. Unitarian Universalist Religious Naturalists. http://uurn.org/.

40. http://thegreatstory.org/.

Bibliography

Altman, Simon. *Is Nature Supernatural?* Amherst, NY: Prometheus Books, 2002.

Amery, Jean. *At the Mind's Limits.* New York: Schocken Books, 1998.

Anderson, P. W. (1972), "More Is Different." *Science* 77 (1972): 393–96.

Aristotle. *Nichomachean Ethics.* Trans. Martin Ostwand. New York: Bobbs-Merrill, 1962.

Atran, Scott. *In Gods We Trust.* New York: Oxford University Press, 2002.

Barnam, James. "Biofunctional Realism and the Problem of Teleology." *Evolution and Cognition* 6 (2000): 23–34.

Belshaw, Christopher. *10 Good Questions About Life and Death.* Oxford: Blackwell, 2005.

Braxton, Donald. "Natural, Supernatural, and Transcendence." *Zygon* 41:2 (2006): 347–63.

Brown, Deborah. *Descartes and the Passionate Mind.* Cambridge: Cambridge University Press, 2006.

Buller, David, ed. *Function, Selection, and Design.* Albany: State University of New York Press, 1999.

Chaisson, Eric. *Epic of Evolution.* New York: Columbia University Press, 2006.

Churchland, Paul. "Eliminative Materialism and the Propositional Attitudes." *The Journal of Philosophy* 78:2 (1981): 67–90.

Clayton, Philip. *Mind and Emergence.* New York: Oxford University Press, 2004.

———, ed. *The Oxford Handbook of Religion and Science.* New York: Oxford University Press, 2006.

———, and Paul Davies, eds. *The Re-Emergence of Emergence.* New York: Oxford University Press, 2006.

Cobb, John B. *A Christian Natural Theology.* Philadelphia: Westminster Press, 1965.

Crosby, Donald. *A Religion of Nature.* Albany: State University of New York Press, 2002.

———. *Living With Ambiguity.* Albany: State University of New York Press, 2008.

Davis, Martin. "The Philosophy of Mind." In *Philosophy,* ed. A. C. Grayling, 250–335. New York: Oxford University Press, 1995.

Dawkins, Richard. *The Blind Watchmaker.* New York: W. W. Norton, 1987.

Deacon, Terrence. *The Symbolic Species.* New York: W. W. Norton, 1997.

———. "Emergence: The Hole at the Wheel's Hub." In *The Re-Emergence of Emergence,* ed. Philip Clayton and Paul Davies, 853–71. New York: Oxford University Press, 2006.

———, and Ursula Goodenough. "The Sacred Emergence of Nature." In *The Oxford Handbook of Religion and Science,* ed. Philip Clayton. New York: Oxford University Press, 2006.

De Duve, Christian. *Vital Dust.* New York: Basic Books, 1995.

Dennett, Daniel. *Darwin's Dangerous Idea.* New York: Simon and Schuster, 1995.

Descartes, René. *The Philosophical Writings of Descartes.* Trans. John Cottingham et al. Cambridge: Cambridge University Press, 1988.

Dostoyevsky, Fyodor. *The Brothers Karamazov.* Translated by Constance Garrett. New York: W. W. Norton, 1976.

Dowd, Michael. *Thank God for Evolution.* New York: Plume, 2007.

Dunlap, Thomas. *Faith in Nature.* Seattle: University of Washington Press, 2004.

Eagleton, Terry. *The Meaning of Life.* Oxford: Oxford University Press, 2007.

Eliade, Mircea. *The Sacred and the Profane.* New York: Harcourt, Brace, and World, 1957.

Freeman, Anthony, ed. *The Emergence of Consciousness.* Charlottesville, VA: Imprint Academic, 2001.

Goodenough, Ursula. *The Sacred Depths of Nature.* New York: Oxford University Press, 1998.

Gottlieb, Roger. *A Spirituality of Resistance.* New York: Crossroad Publishing, 1999.

Guthrie, W. K. C. *The Presocratic Tradition from Parmenides to Democritus.* Cambridge: Cambridge University Press, 1965.

———. *The Sophists.* Cambridge: Cambridge University Press, 1971.

Haught, John. *Is Nature Enough?* Cambridge: Cambridge University Press, 2006.

Hobbes, Thomas. *Leviathan.* London: Penguin Books, 1968.

Holland, John. *Emergence: From Chaos to Order.* New York: Basic Books, 1998.

Hull, David, and Michael Ruse, eds. *The Philosophy of Biology.* New York: Cambridge University Press, 2007.

Illetterati, Luca, and Francesca Michelini, eds. *Purposiveness: Teleology Between Nature and Mind.* Frankfurt: Ontos Verlag, 2008.

Johnson, Steven. *Emergence.* New York: Scribner's, 2001.

Kauffman, Stuart. *The Origins of Order.* New York: Oxford University Press, 1993.

———. *Reinventing the Sacred.* New York: Basic Books, 2008.

Kaufman, Gordon. *In the Beginning . . . Creativity.* Minneapolis: Augsburg Fortress, 2004.

Kerferd, G. B. *The Sophistic Movement.* Cambridge: Cambridge University Press, 1981.

Kierkegaard, Søren. *Concluding Unscientific Postscript to Philosophical Fragments.* Trans. Howard Hong and Edna Hong. Princeton: Princeton University Press, 1992.

Kirk, G. S., J. E. Raven, and M. Schofield. *The Presocratic Philosophers.* Cambridge: Cambridge University Press, 1983.

Klemke, E. D., ed. *The Meaning of Life.* New York: Oxford University Press, 2000.

Laughlin, Robert. *A Different Universe*. New York: Basic Books, 2000.

Macy, Joanna. "Our Life As Gaia." In *Thinking Like a Mountain*, ed. John Seed and Joanna Macy. East Haven, CT: New Society Publishers, 1988.

Marshall, John. *Descartes's Moral Theory*. Ithaca: Cornell University Press, 1998.

Millikan, Ruth. "In Defense of Proper Functions." *Philosophy of Science* 56 (1998): 288–302.

———. *Varieties of Meaning*. Cambridge: MIT Press, 2004.

Moore, G. E. *Principia Ethica*. Cambridge: Cambridge University Press, 1903.

Morowitz, Harold. *The Emergence of Everything*. New York: Oxford University Press, 2002.

Nagel, Thomas. *The View from Nowhere*. New York: Oxford University Press, 1986.

———. "The Absurd." In *The Meaning of Life*, ed. E. D. Klemke, 176–85. New York: Oxford University Press, 2000.

Oates, David. *Earth Rising*. Corvallis: Oregon State University Press, 1989.

Peters, Karl. *Dancing with the Sacred*. Harrisburg, PA: Trinity Press International, 2002.

Pinker, Steven. *The Blank Slate*. New York: Viking, 2002.

Plato. *Complete Works*. Ed. John M. Cooper. Indianapolis: Hackett, 1997.

Raymo, Chet. *When God Is Gone Everything Is Holy*. Notre Dame, IN: Sorin Books, 2008.

Rorty, Richard. *Contingency, Irony, and Solidarity*. Cambridge: Cambridge University Press, 1989.

Rottschaefer, William. *The Biology and Psychology of Moral Agency*. New York: Cambridge University Press, 1998.

Rue, Loyal. *Everybody's Story*. Albany: State University of New York Press, 1999.

———. *Religion Is Not About God*. New Brunswick: Rutgers University Press, 2005.

Ryn, Zdzislaw, and Stanislav Klodzinski. "At the Borderline Between Life and Death." In *Auschwitz-Hefte*, vol. 1. Basel: Beltz, 1987.

Sartre, Jean-Paul. "Existentialism Is a Humanism." In *Existentialism From Dostoevsky to Sartre*, ed. Walter Kaufman. New York: Meridian Books, 1956.

Searle, John. *The Rediscovery of the Mind*. Cambridge: MIT Press, 1992.

Skofsky, Wolfgang. *The Order of Terror: The Concentration Camp*. Trans. William Templer. Princeton: Princeton University Press, 1997.

Stamos, David. *Evolution and the Big Questions*. Malden, MA: Blackwell, 2008.

Stone, Jerome. *Religious Naturalism Today*. Albany: State University of New York Press, 2008.

Swimme, Brian. "Cosmogenesis." In *Worldviews and Ecology*, ed. Mary Evelyn Tucker and John Grim. Maryknoll, NY: Orbis Books, 1994.

Thompson, Garrett. *On the Meaning of Life*. Florence, KY: Wadsworth, 2003.

Tucker, M. T., and John Grim, eds. *Worldviews and Ecology*. Maryknoll, NY: Orbis Books, 1994.

Walter, Alex. "The Anti-Naturalistic Fallacy: Evolutionary Moral Psychology and the Insistence of Brute Facts." *Evolutionary Psychology*, 44 (2006): 33–48.

Wattles, Jeffrey. "Teleology Past and Present." *Zygon* 41:2 (2006): 445–64.

Weinberg, Steven. *The First Three Minutes*. New York: Basic Books, 1977.

———. *Dreams of a Final Theory*. New York: Pantheon Books, 1992.

Whitehead, Alfred N. *The Concept of Nature*. Cambridge: Cambridge University Press, 1920.

———. *Science and the Modern World*. New York: The Free Press, 1925.

———. *Process and Reality*. New York: Macmillan Publishing Co., 1929.

———. *Modes of Thought*. New York: Macmillan Publishing Co., 1938.

Wittgenstein, Ludwig. *Tractatus Logico-Philosophicus*. Trans. C. K. Ogden. London: Routledge and Kegan Paul, 1981.

Wong, Paul, and Prem Fry, eds. *The Human Quest for Meaning*. Mahway, NJ: Lawrence Erlbaum Associates, 1998.

Wright, Robert. *Non-Zero*. New York: Pantheon, 2000.

Index